EP Math
Algebra 1
Quizzes

Easy Peasy

All-in-One
Homeschool

ISBN: 9798516688034

Contents

EP Math Algebra 1 First Quarter Grade

Quiz	Score	Notes	Quiz	Score	Notes
1	/ 5		22	/ 5	
2	/ 5		23	/ 5	
3	/ 5		24	/ 5	
4	/ 5		25	/ 5	
5	/ 5		26	/ 5	
6	/ 5		27	/ 5	
7	/ 5		28		Extra credit
8	/ 5		29	/ 5	
9	/ 5		30	/ 5	
10	/ 5		31	/ 5	
11	/ 5		32	/ 5	
12	/ 5		33	/ 5	
13		Extra credit	34	/ 5	
14	/ 5		35	/ 5	
15	/ 5		36	/ 5	
16	/ 5		37		Extra credit
17	/ 5		38	/ 5	
18	/ 5		39	/ 5	
19	/ 5		40	/ 5	
20	/ 5		41	/ 5	
21		Extra credit	42	/ 5	
			43		Extra credit

Add up all the quiz scores including extra credit, then determine your grade using the table below.

1st Quarter Total	Grade
171 and above	A
152 to less than 171	B
133 to less than 152	C
114 to less than 133	D
Below 114	F

1st Quarter Total

1st Quarter Grade

Total Possible: 190

Extra Credit: 25

EP Math Algebra 1 Second Quarter Grade

Quiz	Score	Notes	Quiz	Score	Notes
48	/ 5		68	/ 5	
49	/ 5		69	/ 5	
50	/ 5		70		Extra credit
51	/ 5		71	/ 5	
52	/ 5		72	/ 5	
53	/ 5		73	/ 5	
54	/ 5		74	/ 5	
55		Extra credit	75	/ 5	
56	/ 5		76	/ 5	
57	/ 5		77	/ 5	
58	/ 5		78	/ 5	
59	/ 5		79		Extra credit
60	/ 5		80	/ 5	
61	/ 5		81	/ 5	
62		Extra credit	82	/ 5	
63	/ 5		83	/ 5	
64	/ 5		84	/ 5	
65	/ 5		85	/ 5	
66	/ 5		86	/ 5	
67	/ 5		87		Extra credit

Add up all the quiz scores including extra credit, then determine your grade using the table below.

2nd Quarter Total	Grade
158 and above	A
140 to less than 158	B
123 to less than 140	C
105 to less than 123	D
Below 105	F

2nd Quarter Total	2nd Quarter Grade

Total Possible: 175
Extra Credit: 25

EP Math Algebra 1 Third Quarter Grade

Quiz	Score	Notes	Quiz	Score	Notes
93	/ 5		113	/ 5	
94	/ 5		114		Extra credit
95	/ 5		115	/ 5	
96	/ 5		116	/ 5	
97	/ 5		117	/ 5	
98	/ 5		118	/ 5	
99	/ 5		119	/ 5	
100	/ 5		120	/ 5	
101	/ 5		121	/ 5	
102		Extra credit	122	/ 5	
103	/ 5		123	/ 5	
104	/ 5		124		Extra credit
105	/ 5		125	/ 5	
106	/ 5		126	/ 5	
107	/ 5		127	/ 5	
108	/ 5		128	/ 5	
109	/ 5		129	/ 5	
110	/ 5		130	/ 5	
111	/ 5		131		Extra credit
112	/ 5				

Add up all the quiz scores including extra credit, then determine your grade using the table below.

3rd Quarter Total	Grade
158 and above	A
140 to less than 158	B
123 to less than 140	C
105 to less than 123	D
Below 105	F

3rd Quarter Total

3rd Quarter Grade

Total Possible: 175
Extra Credit: 20

EP Math Algebra 1 Fourth Quarter Grade

Quiz	Score	Notes	Quiz	Score	Notes
138	/ 5		158	/ 5	
139	/ 5		159	/ 5	
140	/ 5		160	/ 5	
141	/ 5		161	/ 5	
142	/ 5		162	/ 5	
143	/ 5		163	/ 5	
144	/ 5		164	/ 5	
145		Extra credit	165	/ 5	
146	/ 5		166	/ 5	
147	/ 5		167	/ 5	
148	/ 5		168	/ 5	
149	/ 5		169	/ 5	
150	/ 5		170	/ 5	
151	/ 5		171	/ 5	
152	/ 5		172	/ 5	
153	/ 5		173	/ 5	
154	/ 5		174	/ 5	
155		Extra credit	175	/ 5	

Add up all the quiz scores including extra credit, then determine your grade using the table below.

4th Quarter Total	Grade
153 and above	A
136 to less than 153	B
119 to less than 136	C
102 to less than 119	D
Below 102	F

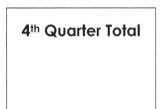

4th Quarter Total

Total Possible: 170
Extra Credit: 10

4th Quarter Grade

EP Math Algebra 1 Course Grade

1st Quarter Total Score	2nd Quarter Total Score	3rd Quarter Total Score	4th Quarter Total Score	Final Exam Score

Add up all the five scores above, then determine your grade using the table below.

Course Total	Grade
675 and above	A
600 to less than 675	B
525 to less than 600	C
450 to less than 525	D
Below 450	F

Course Total	Course Grade

Total Possible: 750
Extra Credit: 80

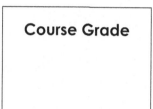

EP Math Algebra 1 Course Grade, Including Participation

Optionally, up to half of your grade could be for participation. Award yourself up to 750 points for completing the daily assignments. Add your participation score to the course total above, then determine your grade using the table below.

Course Total	Grade
1350 and above	A
1200 to less than 1350	B
1050 to less than 1200	C
900 to less than 1050	D
Below 900	F

Course Total	Course Grade

Total Possible: 1500
Extra Credit: 80

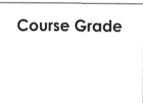

Congratulations!
You completed the course!

This page is intentionally left blank.

LESSON 46 PSAT Practice   Date: _____   Score: _____

1. Ⓐ Ⓑ Ⓒ Ⓓ   6. Ⓐ Ⓑ Ⓒ Ⓓ   11. Ⓐ Ⓑ Ⓒ Ⓓ   16. Ⓐ Ⓑ Ⓒ Ⓓ
2. Ⓐ Ⓑ Ⓒ Ⓓ   7. Ⓐ Ⓑ Ⓒ Ⓓ   12. Ⓐ Ⓑ Ⓒ Ⓓ   17. Ⓐ Ⓑ Ⓒ Ⓓ
3. Ⓐ Ⓑ Ⓒ Ⓓ   8. Ⓐ Ⓑ Ⓒ Ⓓ   13. Ⓐ Ⓑ Ⓒ Ⓓ
4. Ⓐ Ⓑ Ⓒ Ⓓ   9. Ⓐ Ⓑ Ⓒ Ⓓ   14. Ⓐ Ⓑ Ⓒ Ⓓ
5. Ⓐ Ⓑ Ⓒ Ⓓ   10. Ⓐ Ⓑ Ⓒ Ⓓ   15. Ⓐ Ⓑ Ⓒ Ⓓ

Cut Here

LESSON 47 PSAT Practice   Date: _____   Score: _____

1. Ⓐ Ⓑ Ⓒ Ⓓ   6. Ⓐ Ⓑ Ⓒ Ⓓ   11. Ⓐ Ⓑ Ⓒ Ⓓ   16. Ⓐ Ⓑ Ⓒ Ⓓ
2. Ⓐ Ⓑ Ⓒ Ⓓ   7. Ⓐ Ⓑ Ⓒ Ⓓ   12. Ⓐ Ⓑ Ⓒ Ⓓ   17. Ⓐ Ⓑ Ⓒ Ⓓ
3. Ⓐ Ⓑ Ⓒ Ⓓ   8. Ⓐ Ⓑ Ⓒ Ⓓ   13. Ⓐ Ⓑ Ⓒ Ⓓ
4. Ⓐ Ⓑ Ⓒ Ⓓ   9. Ⓐ Ⓑ Ⓒ Ⓓ   14. Ⓐ Ⓑ Ⓒ Ⓓ
5. Ⓐ Ⓑ Ⓒ Ⓓ   10. Ⓐ Ⓑ Ⓒ Ⓓ   15. Ⓐ Ⓑ Ⓒ Ⓓ

Cut Here

LESSON 91 PSAT Practice   Date: _____   Score: _____

1. Ⓐ Ⓑ Ⓒ Ⓓ   6. Ⓐ Ⓑ Ⓒ Ⓓ   11. Ⓐ Ⓑ Ⓒ Ⓓ   16. Ⓐ Ⓑ Ⓒ Ⓓ
2. Ⓐ Ⓑ Ⓒ Ⓓ   7. Ⓐ Ⓑ Ⓒ Ⓓ   12. Ⓐ Ⓑ Ⓒ Ⓓ   17. Ⓐ Ⓑ Ⓒ Ⓓ
3. Ⓐ Ⓑ Ⓒ Ⓓ   8. Ⓐ Ⓑ Ⓒ Ⓓ   13. Ⓐ Ⓑ Ⓒ Ⓓ
4. Ⓐ Ⓑ Ⓒ Ⓓ   9. Ⓐ Ⓑ Ⓒ Ⓓ   14. Ⓐ Ⓑ Ⓒ Ⓓ
5. Ⓐ Ⓑ Ⓒ Ⓓ   10. Ⓐ Ⓑ Ⓒ Ⓓ   15. Ⓐ Ⓑ Ⓒ Ⓓ

Cut Here

This page is intentionally left blank.

LESSON 92 PSAT Practice

Date: _____   Score: _____

1. Ⓐ Ⓑ Ⓒ Ⓓ   6. Ⓐ Ⓑ Ⓒ Ⓓ   11. Ⓐ Ⓑ Ⓒ Ⓓ   16. Ⓐ Ⓑ Ⓒ Ⓓ
2. Ⓐ Ⓑ Ⓒ Ⓓ   7. Ⓐ Ⓑ Ⓒ Ⓓ   12. Ⓐ Ⓑ Ⓒ Ⓓ   17. Ⓐ Ⓑ Ⓒ Ⓓ
3. Ⓐ Ⓑ Ⓒ Ⓓ   8. Ⓐ Ⓑ Ⓒ Ⓓ   13. Ⓐ Ⓑ Ⓒ Ⓓ
4. Ⓐ Ⓑ Ⓒ Ⓓ   9. Ⓐ Ⓑ Ⓒ Ⓓ   14. Ⓐ Ⓑ Ⓒ Ⓓ
5. Ⓐ Ⓑ Ⓒ Ⓓ   10. Ⓐ Ⓑ Ⓒ Ⓓ   15. Ⓐ Ⓑ Ⓒ Ⓓ

Cut Here

LESSON 136 PSAT Practice

Date: _____   Score: _____

1. Ⓐ Ⓑ Ⓒ Ⓓ   6. Ⓐ Ⓑ Ⓒ Ⓓ   11. Ⓐ Ⓑ Ⓒ Ⓓ   16. Ⓐ Ⓑ Ⓒ Ⓓ
2. Ⓐ Ⓑ Ⓒ Ⓓ   7. Ⓐ Ⓑ Ⓒ Ⓓ   12. Ⓐ Ⓑ Ⓒ Ⓓ   17. Ⓐ Ⓑ Ⓒ Ⓓ
3. Ⓐ Ⓑ Ⓒ Ⓓ   8. Ⓐ Ⓑ Ⓒ Ⓓ   13. Ⓐ Ⓑ Ⓒ Ⓓ
4. Ⓐ Ⓑ Ⓒ Ⓓ   9. Ⓐ Ⓑ Ⓒ Ⓓ   14. Ⓐ Ⓑ Ⓒ Ⓓ
5. Ⓐ Ⓑ Ⓒ Ⓓ   10. Ⓐ Ⓑ Ⓒ Ⓓ   15. Ⓐ Ⓑ Ⓒ Ⓓ

Cut Here

LESSON 137 PSAT Practice

Date: _____   Score: _____

1. Ⓐ Ⓑ Ⓒ Ⓓ   6. Ⓐ Ⓑ Ⓒ Ⓓ   11. Ⓐ Ⓑ Ⓒ Ⓓ   16. Ⓐ Ⓑ Ⓒ Ⓓ
2. Ⓐ Ⓑ Ⓒ Ⓓ   7. Ⓐ Ⓑ Ⓒ Ⓓ   12. Ⓐ Ⓑ Ⓒ Ⓓ   17. Ⓐ Ⓑ Ⓒ Ⓓ
3. Ⓐ Ⓑ Ⓒ Ⓓ   8. Ⓐ Ⓑ Ⓒ Ⓓ   13. Ⓐ Ⓑ Ⓒ Ⓓ
4. Ⓐ Ⓑ Ⓒ Ⓓ   9. Ⓐ Ⓑ Ⓒ Ⓓ   14. Ⓐ Ⓑ Ⓒ Ⓓ
5. Ⓐ Ⓑ Ⓒ Ⓓ   10. Ⓐ Ⓑ Ⓒ Ⓓ   15. Ⓐ Ⓑ Ⓒ Ⓓ

Cut Here

This page is intentionally left blank.

Quiz 1 ···

1. What is the first step in evaluating the expression $5 + (2 - 4 \times 3)^2$?

   A) Addition

   B) Subtraction

   C) Multiplication

   D) Exponent

Evaluate.

2. $3 + 16 \div 4$

3. $4 \times 7 - 2 \times 6 \div 3$

4. $5^2 - 4 \times (2^3 - 3)$

5. $(-3)^4 \div 9 \times (4 - 5)^3 + 8$

Quiz 2 ···

Evaluate.

1. $4x + 7$ for $x = -2$

2. $x^2 - 4xy + 4y^2$ for $x = 5$ and $y = 4$

Simplify.

3. $2x - 3 - x + 5$

4. $5(x + 1) - 2(4 - x)$

5. $x - 3(x^2 - x) + 5x + x^2$

Quiz 3 ··

1. What is the first step in solving the equation $2x - 1 = 3$?

    A) Add 1 to both sides.

    B) Subtract 3 from both sides.

    C) Divide both sides by 2.

    D) Divide both sides by 3.

Solve.

2. $x + 4 = 10$

3. $-7x = 63$

4. $5x + 4 = 19$

5. $9 - 3x = 24$

Quiz 4 ···

Solve. Reduce fractions but leave them improper.

1. $2x + 1 = 7x + 3$

2. $3x + 2 - x = 5 - 2x + 3$

3. $8 = 3 - 4(x - 3)$

4. $6(x - 2) + 5 = 4x - 5$

5. $-4(x + 1) + 3x = 2(x - 3)$

Quiz 5 ⋯⋯⋯⋯⋯⋯⋯⋯⋯⋯⋯⋯⋯⋯⋯⋯⋯⋯⋯⋯⋯⋯⋯⋯⋯⋯⋯⋯

1. $\dfrac{1}{2}x + \dfrac{1}{4} = \dfrac{2}{3}$

   What is the least common denominator of all the fractions in the equation above?

Solve. Reduce fractions but leave them improper.

2. $0.3x - 1.2 = -0.5x + 0.4$

3. $0.02x + 0.25 = -0.03x - 0.5$

4. $\dfrac{3}{4}x + \dfrac{1}{5} = \dfrac{1}{2}x + \dfrac{2}{5}$

5. $\dfrac{1}{2}(3x + 1) = 2x + \dfrac{3}{4}$

Quiz 6 ···

Solve. Reduce fractions but leave them improper.

1. $|3x| = 21$

2. $|x - 7| = 5$

3. $|4x + 1| + 3 = 8$

4. $9 - 3|x - 2| = 4$

5. $5|2x + 3| + 6 = 21$

Quiz 7 ·· EP Math Algebra 1 Quizzes

Solve. Reduce fractions but leave them improper.

1. $2x + 3 = 9$

2. $2x - 1 = 5 - 6x$

3. $5x + 4 = 7 - 2(x + 1)$

4. $\dfrac{1}{6}x + \dfrac{2}{9} = x - \dfrac{1}{3}$

5. $17 - 5|2x - 3| = -8$

Quiz 8 ··

Solve. Reduce fractions but leave them improper.

1. $x + 3 = x + 5$

2. $2x - 5 = 3x - 2x$

3. $4(3x + 2) - x = 11x + 8$

4. $|4x - 7| + 9 = 3$

5. $3|x + 4| - 15 = 0$

Quiz 9 ···

1. The sum of two consecutive even integers is 54. What are the two integers?

2. The length of a rectangle is 5 feet less than three times its width. The perimeter is 30 feet. What are the dimensions of the rectangle?

3. Luke has $1.40 in quarters and nickels. He has 2 more quarters than nickels. How many coins of each type does he have?

4. Jennifer and her friends went out for dinner. They paid a total of $60 for their meal, including a tip of 20%. What was the cost of the meal before the tip?

5. Michael is 4 years older than Emma. Five years ago, the sum of their ages was 20. How old are they now?

Quiz 10 ··

1. How long in hours will it take to travel 195 miles at an average speed of 65 mph?

2. It takes 20 minutes to drive to a mall at 30 mph. How long in minutes will it take to drive to the mall at 40 mph?

3. Eli and Alex began jogging from the same spot at the same time in opposite directions on a 12-mile circular trail. Eli runs at 4 mph, and Alex at 6 mph. How long will it take them to meet?

4. Arthur walked around a circular trail twice in a total of 4.5 hours. He walked the circle at 4 mph the first time and at 5 mph the second time. How long is the trail?

5. Olivia began cycling a trail at 10 mph. An hour later, Lucas began cycling the trail from the same point in the same direction at 14 mph. How long will it take for Lucas to catch up with Olivia?

Quiz 11 ·· ·

1. How many grams of salt is in 30 grams of a 20% saline solution?

2. How many grams of water must be mixed with 10 grams of salt to produce a 25% saline solution?

3. How many ounces of a 10% acid solution must be added to 6 ounces of a 15% acid solution to produce a 12% acid solution?

4. Two pounds of nuts costing $4 per pound are mixed with 3 pounds of nuts costing $6 per pound. What is the price of the mixture per pound?

5. Peanuts cost $3 per pound. Cashews cost $5 per pound. How many pounds of peanuts must be mixed with 6 pounds of cashews to make a mixture of nuts that costs $4.50 per pound?

Quiz 12 ···

Solve for y.

1. $2x - 1 = x - y$

2. $3(x + y) = 4y + 5$

3. $\dfrac{1}{3}y + \dfrac{5}{6}x = x - \dfrac{2}{3}$

Solve for the specified variable.

4. The formula $P = 2l + 2w$ gives the perimeter P of a rectangle with width w and length l. Solve the formula for w.

5. The formula $F = \dfrac{9}{5}C + 32$ gives the Fahrenheit temperature F for a given Celsius temperature C. Solve the formula for C.

Quiz 13 ···

Evaluate.

1. $6 + (3 \times 2^3 - 4^2 \div 4^1) \div 5$

Solve. Reduce fractions but leave them improper.

2. $6x - 4 = 11$

3. $4(x - 3) + 2x = 3x - 8$

4. $3|2x + 5| - 7 = 8$

5. Two trains leave a station at the same time and travel in opposite directions. One train travels at 110 mph while the other travels at 120 mph. How long does it take for the two trains to be 920 miles apart?

Quiz 14 ···

1. Which statement is true?

   A) $(0, -3)$ is a solution to $y = x + 3$.

   B) $(-4, 2)$ is a solution to $y = x + 2$.

   C) $(2, -1)$ is a solution to $x + 2y = 0$.

   D) $(-1, 0)$ is a solution to $3x - y = 1$.

Complete the table of x and y values given the equation.

2. $y = 2x - 3$

x	-2	0			6
y			1	5	

3. $3x + 2y = 4$

x		-2	0		
y	8			-1	-4

Graph by plotting at least three points.

4. $y = 2x + 1$

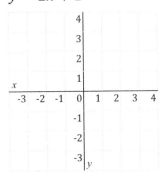

5. $2x + 3y = 6$

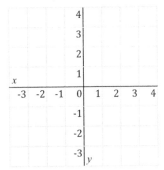

Quiz 15 ·· EP Math Algebra 1 Quizzes · 29

Find the slope of the line given its graph or given two points on the line.

1.

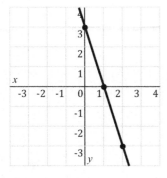

2. $(-2, 2)$ and $(1, 8)$

3. $(3, 10)$ and $(6, -2)$

4. $(2, 4)$ and $(-8, 0)$

5. $(4, 9)$ and $(-4, 5)$

Quiz 16 ···

Find the slope and *y*-intercept.

1. $y = -x + 5$

2. $y = \dfrac{1}{4}x - 3$

Graph using the slope and *y*-intercept.

3. $y = x - 2$

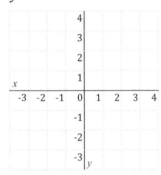

4. $y = -2x + 3$

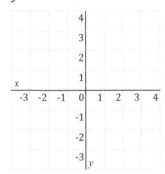

5. $y = \dfrac{3}{4}x + 1$

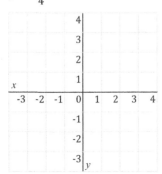

Quiz 17 ··· EP Math Algebra 1

Find the slope and y-intercept.

1. $x - y = 5$

2. $x + 2y = 8$

Graph using the slope and y-intercept.

3. $4x + y = 1$

4. $x - 3y = 3$

5. $3x - 2y = -4$

Quiz 18 ··

Find the x-intercept and y-intercept.

1. $x - 2y = 6$

2. $5x + 3y = 15$

Graph using the x-intercept and y-intercept.

3. $3x + y = 3$

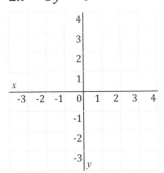

4. $2x - 3y = 6$

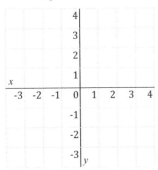

5. $4x + 3y = -12$

Quiz 19 ···

1. Write an equation of a line that is vertical and passes through $(3, 4)$.

2. Write an equation of a line that is horizontal and has a y-intercept of -2.

Determine if the lines are parallel, perpendicular, or neither.

3. $y = 5x + 4$
   $x + 5y = 2$

4. $3x + 4y = 0$
   $y = -3x + 4$

5. $2x + 3y = 3$
   $4x + 6y = -4$

Quiz 20 ··

Graph by plotting the vertex and two additional points.

1. $y = |x + 2|$

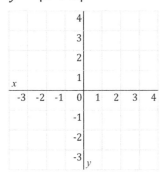

2. $y = -|x - 1| + 3$

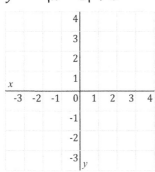

Find the vertex of the graph, then determine whether the graph opens up or down.

3. $y = |x| - 5$

4. $y = -|x + 3|$

5. $y = |x - 4| + 2$

Quiz 21 ···

1. Find the slope of a line passing through $(3, 7)$ and $(-2, 4)$.

2. Find the slope of a line perpendicular to the line passing through $(4, 5)$ and $(-2, 3)$.

3. Write an equation of a line that is parallel to the y-axis and has an x-intercept of 4.

Graph using any method.

4. $x + 2y = 4$

5. $y = |x + 1| - 3$

Quiz 22

Find an equation of each line in slope-intercept form.

1.
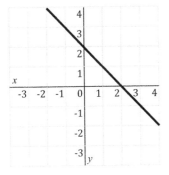

2.
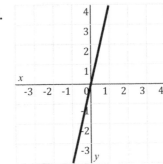

3.
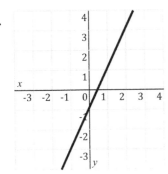

4.
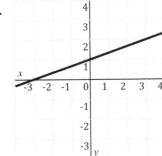

5.
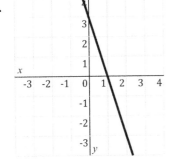

Quiz 23 .... ·

Find an equation of each line in slope-intercept form.

1. A line has a slope of -1 and passes through $(8, -3)$.

2. A line passes through $(-2, -6)$ and $(1, 9)$.

3. A line passes through $(-5, 3)$ and $(10, 3)$.

4. A line is parallel to $2x + y = 0$ and passes through $(6, -7)$.

5. A line is perpendicular to $4x - 3y = 6$ and passes through $(8, -4)$.

Quiz 24 ···

Find an equation of each line in point-slope form. Use the first point when given two points.

1. A line has a slope of 4 and passes through $(2, 7)$.

2. A line passes through $(-3, -1)$ and $(-4, 4)$.

3. A line passes through $(-5, 8)$ and $(3, 0)$.

4. A line is parallel to $x - 2y = 6$ and passes through $(6, -4)$.

5. A line is perpendicular to $x + 3y = 1$ and passes through $(-5, -8)$.

Quiz 25 ···

Find an equation of each line in standard form. Use only integers and the smallest possible positive integer coefficient for x.

1. A line has a slope of -3 and passes through $(-1, 5)$.

2. A line passes through $(-6, 3)$ and $(4, -1)$.

3. A line passes through $(7, 0)$ and $(-5, -2)$.

4. A line is parallel to $x = -6$ and passes through $(3, -4)$.

5. A line is perpendicular to $3x + 2y = 4$ and passes through $(5, 5)$.

Quiz 26 ···

Solve.

1. A canoe rental shop charges a $10 fixed fee plus $8 per hour for renting a canoe. Write an equation representing the total cost, y, of renting a canoe for x hours. How much will it cost to rent a canoe for 4 hours?

2. A plumber charges $30 for a service call plus $42 per hour of service. Write an equation representing the total cost, y, after x hours of service. How much will it cost for a job that takes 3 hours?

3. An empty water tank is being filled at a rate of 7 gallons per minute. Write an equation representing the amount of water, y, in the tank after x minutes. How much water will be in the tank after 15 minutes?

4. Rachel joined a gym that charges a $50 joining fee plus $24 per month. She also rented a locker at $6 per month. Write an equation representing Rachel's total cost, y, of joining the gym for x months. How much will she pay for 6 months?

5. A submarine 1,500 feet below the surface of the water begins ascending at an average speed of 60 feet per minute. Write an equation representing the depth, y, of the submarine after x minutes. How long will it take the submarine to reach the surface of the water?

Quiz 27 ·· ·····

Solve.

1. Hailey has x five-dollar bills and y one-dollar bills amounting to $64. Write an equation relating x and y. If she has 9 ones, how many fives does she have?

2. Watermelons cost $6 each. Mangos cost $2 each. Sue has $30 to buy x watermelons and y mangos. Write an equation relating x and y. If Sue buys 3 watermelons, how many mangos can she buy?

3. A 100-point test has x questions worth 4 points each and y questions worth 8 points each. Write an equation relating x and y. If there are 11 questions worth 4 points each, how many questions will be worth 8 points each?

4. A group of x adults and y children paid a total of $98 for movie tickets. Adult tickets cost $12 each and child tickets cost $10 each. Write an equation relating x and y. If they bought 4 adult tickets, how many child tickets did they buy?

5. A restaurant has x tables that seat 2 people and y tables that seat 6 people. The restaurant can seat a total of 78 people. Write an equation relating x and y. If 15 tables seat 2 people, how many tables seat 6 people?

Quiz 28 ···

Find an equation of each line in standard form. Use only integers and the smallest possible positive integer coefficient for x.

1.

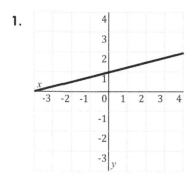

2. A line has a slope of -3 and passes through $(5, -7)$.

3. A line passes through $(-2, 3)$ and $(4, -1)$.

4. A line is perpendicular to $x - 2y = 3$ and passes through $(-6, 5)$.

Solve.

5. A plane 7,000 feet above the ground begins descending at an average speed of 500 feet per minute. Write an equation representing the altitude, y, of the plane after x minutes. How long will it take the plane to reach an altitude of 2,500 feet?

Quiz 29 ···

1. $2x + y = 6$

   $x - 4y = 12$

   $3x + 2y = 8$

   Which of the following is the solution to the system of equations above?

   A) $(3, 0)$ B) $(8, -1)$ C) $(4, -2)$ D) $(-2, 7)$

Solve by graphing.

2. $x = 2$ and $y = 3x - 4$

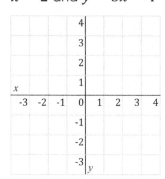

3. $y = x - 2$ and $y = -2x + 1$

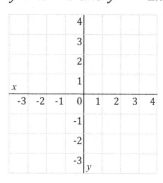

4. $5x + y = 3$ and $2x + 3y = 9$

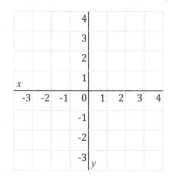

5. $x - 3y = 4$ and $3x + y = -8$

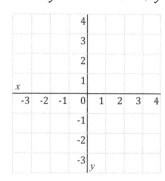

Quiz 30 ···

Solve by substitution.

1. $y = 3x + 2$
   $x + 6y = 12$

2. $y = 4x - 1$
   $5x - 4y = -7$

3. $x + 3y = -9$
   $3x - 2y = -5$

4. $x - 2y = 13$
   $x + 5y = -15$

5. $6x + 2y = 4$
   $2x - 3y = 27$

Quiz 31 ·· 45

Solve by elimination.

1. $x + 8y = 13$
   $x - 2y = -7$

2. $3x - y = 15$
   $5x + 2y = -8$

3. $2x + 6y = 0$
   $3x + 2y = -14$

4. $3x + 4y = -9$
   $4x - 3y = 13$

5. $2x - 5y = -30$
   $3x + 10y = 25$

Quiz 32 ···

Solve using any method.

1. $y = -x + 8$
   $x - 9y = 8$

2. $3x + 2y = 14$
   $5x - 2y = 18$

3. $4x + 5y = 8$
   $2x + 7y = -14$

4. $3x - y = 12$
   $6x + 5y = 3$

5. $2x + 7y = 25$
   $4x - 6y = 30$

Quiz 33 $\cdots\cdots\cdots\cdots\cdots\cdots\cdots\cdots\cdots\cdots\cdots\cdots\cdots\cdots\cdots\cdots\cdots\cdots\cdots\cdots\cdots\cdots\cdots\cdots\cdots$

1. A system of linear equations has no solution if

   A) the lines have different slopes.

   B) the lines have different y-intercepts.

   C) the lines have the same slope but different y-intercepts.

   D) the lines have the same slope and the same y-intercept.

2. Which system of equations has infinitely many solutions?

   A) $x + 3y = -1$ and $2x + 6y = 2$

   B) $y = 2x - 5$ and $4x - 2y = 10$

   C) $x + 2y = 4$ and $4x - y = -2$

   D) $y = -3x + 4$ and $5x + 2y = 8$

Solve using any method.

3. $y = 2x - 9$
   $x + 5y = -1$

4. $5x - y = -7$
   $9x + 2y = 14$

5. $4x + 3y = 11$
   $3x - 2y = 21$

Quiz 34 ··

1. The sum of the digits of a two-digit number is 10. When the digits are reversed, the number is increased by 18. What is the number?

2. Leah has $3.60 in quarters and dimes. She has eight more dimes than quarters. How many of each type of coin does Leah have?

3. The sum of Max and Kate's ages is 32. Seven years ago, Max was twice as old as Kate. How old are they now?

4. A restaurant has 20 tables that can seat a total of 92 people. Some tables seat 4 people and the others seat 6 people. How many tables seat 4 people? How many tables seat 6 people?

5. Six muffins and three cookies cost $10.20. Three muffins and a dozen cookies cost $11.40. How much does a muffin cost, and how much does a cookie cost?

Quiz 35 ···

1. Lynn took two buses to travel 332 km. The first bus averaged 64 km/hr. The second bus averaged 70 km/hr. The whole trip took 5 hours. How much time did she spend in each bus?

2. An airplane flying with the wind traveled 2,700 miles in 9 hours. The return trip took 10 hours flying against the wind. What was the speed of the plane in still air? What was the speed of the wind?

3. A boat takes 4 hours to travel 120 km upstream. The return trip downstream takes only 3 hours. What is the speed of the boat in still water? What is the speed of the current?

4. Two trains leave a station at the same time and travel in opposite directions. One train travels 20 mph faster than the other train. After 3 hours, they are 810 miles apart. What is the speed of each train?

5. Two airplanes leave airports 1,600 miles apart at the same time and travel toward each other. One plane travels 40 mph faster than the other. If they meet after 2.5 hours, what is the speed of each plane?

Quiz 36

1. How much water should be added to 180 liters of a 25% saline solution to make an 18% saline solution?

2. A 20% alcohol solution is to be mixed with a 50% alcohol solution to produce 15 gallons of a 40% alcohol solution. How much of each should be used?

3. A chemist wants to make 30 ounces of a 24% acid solution by mixing a 15% acid solution and a 30% acid solution. How much of each should be used?

4. Coffee A costs $15 per pound. Coffee B costs $12 per pound. How much of each should be mixed to produce 18 pounds of a coffee blend that costs $13 per pound?

5. Walnuts sell for $4.50 a pound. Almonds sells for $6 a pound. A store wants to make 25 pounds of a mixture to sell for $5.10 per pound. How much of each should be used?

Quiz 37 ···

Solve.

1. $x = -4$
   $4x + 7y = 5$

2. $x + 3y = -1$
   $3x - 2y = 19$

3. Movie tickets cost \$12 for adults and \$10 for children. A group bought 9 tickets and paid \$98 in total. How many adults and how many children were in the group?

4. A man in a canoe travels 16 miles downstream in a river in 2 hours. The return trip upstream takes twice as long. Find the average speed of the canoe in still water and the speed of the current.

5. One juice drink is 12% orange juice. Another is 20% pineapple juice. How much of each should be mixed to make 16 ounces of 18% fruit juice?

Quiz 38 ···

1. Graph $x > 4$.

Solve.

2. $7x - 1 \leq -22$

3. $4(3 - 2x) - 2 > 8$

4. $\dfrac{1}{2}x + \dfrac{3}{4} < x - \dfrac{1}{2}$

5. The sum of two consecutive integers is at most 35. What is the greatest possible value for the greater integer?

Quiz 39 ·· EP Math Algebra 1 Quizzes · 53

1. Graph $-3 < x \le 2$.

Solve.

2. $-7 \le 2x + 3 < 11$

3. $-4x \ge 16$ and $3x - 5 < 10$

4. $x - 5(x + 2) > 6$ or $2 + 7x < x + 8$

5. $\dfrac{3}{10} \le \dfrac{1}{2} - \dfrac{3}{5}x < \dfrac{4}{5}$

Quiz 40 ···

1. Graph $|x| \geq 2$.

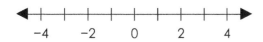

Solve.

2. $|x + 5| \leq 3$

3. $|2x - 5| > 7$

4. $3 + |1 - 2x| \geq 4$

5. $2|4 - x| - 7 < 5$

Quiz 41 ···

1. Which ordered pair is NOT a solution to the inequality $2x + 3y > -6$?

   A) $(4, 2)$ B) $(-6, 3)$ C) $(5, -1)$ D) $(3, -4)$

Graph.

2. $y > 2x + 1$

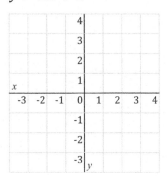

3. $x \le -1$

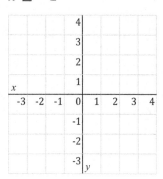

4. $3x - y > 4$

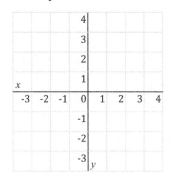

5. $4x + 3y > -6$

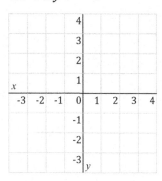

Quiz 42 ···

1. Which system of inequalities has no solution?

   A) $y > 1$ and $x \leq 3$

   B) $y > 1$ and $y < -2$

   C) $x \leq 2$ and $x > -1$

   D) $x \leq 3$ and $x \geq 3$

Which region represents the solution set to the system?

2. $y \geq -x$ and $y < 2x - 3$

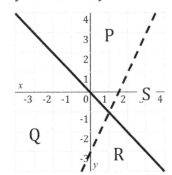

3. $x + 2y < 4$ and $x + 2y > -4$

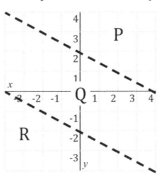

Graph.

4. $x \geq 1$ and $y > -3x + 1$

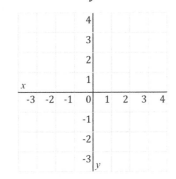

5. $x + y \leq 2$ and $x - 4y < 2$

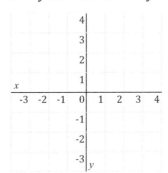

Quiz 43 ·· 57

Solve.

1. $2(x + 3) > x + 4$

2. $-2 \leq 1 - 3x < 10$

3. $|5 - 2x| + 3 > 8$

4. Which inequality is graphed below?

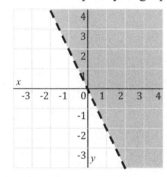

    A) $y < 2x$

    B) $y > 2x$

    C) $y < -2x$

    D) $y > -2x$

5. Which system of inequalities is graphed below?

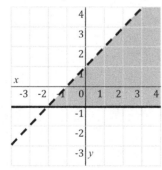

    A) $x \geq -1$ and $x - y > -1$

    B) $x \geq -1$ and $x - y < -1$

    C) $y \geq -1$ and $x - y > -1$

    D) $y \geq -1$ and $x - y < -1$

Quiz 48 ···

Identify as a function or not a function. Explain.

1. $\{(0, 1), (1, 1), (3, 0), (5, -4)\}$

2.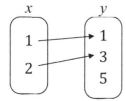

3.

x	2	1	0	1	2
y	-4	-2	0	2	4

4.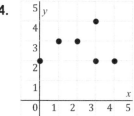

5.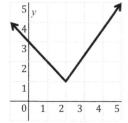

Quiz 49 ···

1. The formula $S = 180(n - 2)$ gives the sum, S, of the interior angle measures of a polygon with n sides. Identify the dependent and independent variables.

Find the domain and range of the relation, then determine if the relation is a function.

2.
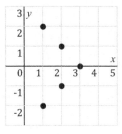

3.
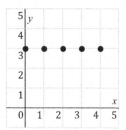

4.
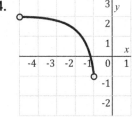

5.
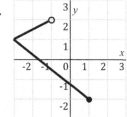

Quiz 50 ···

Find the value(s) of n.

1. $f(x) = x^2 - 7; f(-4) = n$

2. $g(x) = 3x + 5; g(n) = -10$

3. $h(x) = |x| - 4; h(n) = 8$

Find the value(s) of n given the graph of p.

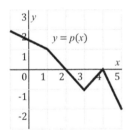

4. $p(4) - p(1) = n$

5. $p(n) = 0$

Quiz 51 ···

1. Which equation is linear?

    A) $x = 5$

    B) $x + y = 5$

    C) $xy = 5$

    D) $x^2 + y = 5$

Identify as linear or nonlinear. If linear, write a rule.

2.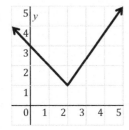

3.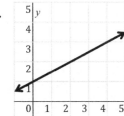

4.

x	−4	−2	0	2	4
y	0	2	4	6	8

5.

x	−2	−1	0	1	2
y	4	1	0	1	4

Quiz 52 ··

1. Which equation is exponential?

   A) $y = 2^x$

   B) $xy = 2$

   C) $y = x^2$

   D) $x + y = 0$

Classify as linear, exponential, or quadratic.

2.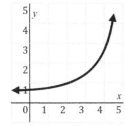

3.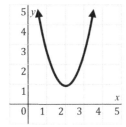

4.

x	−1	0	1	2	3
y	1	3	5	7	9

5.

x	1	2	3	4	5
y	2	4	8	16	32

Quiz 53 ···

Find the average rate of change of f over the given interval.

1. $-1 \leq x \leq 2$

x	-1	0	1	2	3
$f(x)$	1	3	5	7	9

2. $0 \leq x \leq 4$

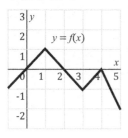

3. $f(x) = 4x + 7; -3 \leq x \leq 6$

4. $f(x) = 2^x; 2 \leq x \leq 6$

Solve.

5. A model rocket is launched straight upward with an initial speed of 160 feet per second. Its height h, in feet, after t seconds is given by the function $h(t) = -16t^2 + 160t$. Find the average rate of change from $t = 0$ to $t = 5$.

Quiz 54 ···

Find the value of n.

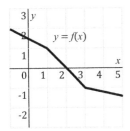

1. $f^{-1}(1) = n$

2. $f^{-1}(-1) = n$

Find the inverse of the function.

3. $f(x) = x - 1$

4. $f(x) = -x + 7$

5. $f(x) = \dfrac{1}{2}x + \dfrac{3}{2}$

Quiz 55 ··· EP Math Algebra 1 Quizzes · 65

1. Does the graph represent a function?

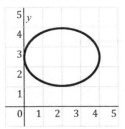

2. Is the table linear or nonlinear?

x	−4	−2	0	2	4
y	2	0	−2	0	2

3. Is the table linear, quadratic, or exponential?

x	0	1	2	3	4
y	1	4	9	16	25

4. What is the average rate of change of $f(x) = x^3$ over the interval $-1 \leq x \leq 2$?

5. If $f(x) = 3x - 6$, what is $f^{-1}(x)$?

Quiz 56 ···

1. Which equation represents direct variation?

   A) $y = 5x$

   B) $xy = 5$

   C) $y = 5$

   D) $x + y = 5$

2. Write a direct variation equation if y varies directly with x and $y = 8$ and $x = 2$.

3. Suppose y varies directly with x, and $y = -9$ when $x = 3$. Find y when $x = -5$.

4. Suppose y varies directly with x, and $y = 1$ when $x = 5$. Find x when $y = 2$.

5. The number of words Emma types varies directly with the time she spends typing. Emma types 80 words in 2 minutes. How many words will she type in 5 minutes?

Quiz 57 ···

1. Which equation represents inverse variation?

   A) $y = 7x$

   B) $xy = 7$

   C) $y = 7$

   D) $x + y = 7$

2. Write an inverse variation equation if y varies inversely with x and $y = 3$ and $x = 2$.

3. Suppose y varies inversely with x, and $y = 10$ when $x = -2$. Find y when $x = 5$.

4. Suppose y varies inversely with x, and $y = 6$ when $x = 2$. Find x when $y = 3$.

5. The time it takes to travel a certain distance varies inversely with the speed traveled. If it takes 20 minutes to drive to work at 60 mph, how long will it take to drive back home at 50 mph?

Quiz 58 ··

1. Write the next two terms of the arithmetic sequence 3, 5, 7, 9, 11, ...

2. Write the first five terms of the arithmetic sequence with $a_1 = 5$ and $d = -3$.

Write a rule for the arithmetic sequence.

3. $a_1 = 10$ and $d = 6$

4. 8, 3, −2, −7, −12, ...

5. 16, 23, 30, 37, 44, ...

Quiz 59 ·· EP Math Algebra 1 Quizzes ···

1. Write the next two terms of the geometric sequence 1, 2, 4, 8, 16, ...

2. Write the first five terms of the geometric sequence with $a_1 = 2$ and $r = 3$.

Write a rule for the geometric sequence.

3. $a_1 = 3$ and $r = 2$

4. 2, 10, 50, 250, 1250, ...

5. 1, −3, 9, −27, 81, ...

Quiz 60 ···

Find the explicit formula.

1. 2, 9, 16, 23, 30, ...

2. 2, 6, 18, 54, 162, ...

Find the recursive formula.

3. 5, 1, −3, −7, −11, ...

4. 5, 10, 20, 40, 80, ...

5. 4, −12, 36, −108, 324, ...

Quiz 61 ···

Find the 8th term.

1. 6, 9, 12, 15, 18, …

2. 1, 2, 4, 8, 16, …

Solve. Use a calculator if necessary. Round your answers to the nearest whole number.

3. A tree grows 0.7 feet per year. It was 4 feet tall at the beginning of this year. What will be the height of the tree at the beginning of the 6th year?

4. As a car gets older, its resale value goes down by 20% each year. Kyle bought a new car for $22,000. What will be the value of the car after 5 years?

5. Ed started a job that paid $68,000 a year. Each year after the first, he received a raise of $1,200. What was Ed's salary in his 9th year of employment?

Quiz 62 ···

1. Suppose y varies directly with x, and $y = 12$ when $x = 4$. Find y when $x = 2$.

2. Suppose y varies inversely with x, and $y = -4$ when $x = -5$. Find x when $y = 2$.

3. Write the explicit formula of the sequence 15, 17, 19, 21, 23, ...

4. Write the recursive formula of the sequence 1, 5, 25, 125, 625, ...

5. During a science experiment, Carol found that bacteria double every hour. There were 20 bacteria at 1 pm. How many bacteria will be there at 6 pm on the same day?

Quiz 63 ·· EP Math Algebra 1 Quizzes · 73

Evaluate.

1. $\sqrt{36}$

2. $\sqrt[3]{-64}$

3. $\sqrt[4]{81}$

4. $\sqrt{144} + \sqrt{16} \times \sqrt[3]{-8}$

5. $\left(\sqrt{25} + \sqrt[3]{27} + \sqrt[5]{32}\right) \times \sqrt{0.04}$

Quiz 64 ··

Simplify.

1. $\sqrt{50}$

2. $\sqrt{27}$

3. $3\sqrt{20}$

4. $2\sqrt{112}$

5. $\sqrt{\dfrac{24}{121}}$

Quiz 65 ··

Simplify. Assume that all variables are positive.

1. $\sqrt{x^2 y^2}$

2. $\sqrt{45x^3}$

3. $2\sqrt{63x^4 y}$

4. $-3\sqrt{18x^2 y^5}$

5. $\sqrt{\dfrac{9}{x^6 y^2 z^4}}$

Quiz 66 ···

Simplify.

1. $4\sqrt{3} - \sqrt{5} + \sqrt{3} + 2\sqrt{5}$

2. $3\sqrt{6} - \sqrt{24}$

3. $\sqrt{32} + \sqrt{18}$

4. $\sqrt{25} - \sqrt{98} + 3\sqrt{32}$

5. $\sqrt{75} + 2\sqrt{45} - 4\sqrt{27} - \sqrt{80}$

Quiz 67 ···

Simplify. Rationalize all denominators. Assume that all variables are positive.

1. $\sqrt{2} \cdot \sqrt{6}$

2. $\sqrt{8x} \cdot \sqrt{5x}$

3. $\sqrt{3x^3y} \cdot \sqrt{12xy}$

4. $\dfrac{3}{\sqrt{7}}$

5. $\dfrac{\sqrt{54x^3}}{\sqrt{2x}}$

Quiz 68 ···

Solve. Check for extraneous solutions.

1. $\sqrt{x} + 2 = 6$

2. $\sqrt{2x - 3} = 1$

3. $2\sqrt{x + 1} = \sqrt{3x + 4}$

4. $\sqrt{5x - 1} = \sqrt{x - 9}$

5. $\sqrt[3]{x + 9} + 4 = 2$

Quiz 69 ···

Solve. Leave your answers in simplest radical form, if applicable.

1. The area of a square is 60 square inches. What is the length of one side?

2. A right triangle has legs with lengths of 3 cm and 4 cm. What is the length of the hypotenuse?

3. An isosceles right triangle has a hypotenuse of $7\sqrt{2}$ cm. What is the length of each leg?

4. A rectangle has a diagonal of 8 inches and a length of 6 inches. What is the width of the rectangle?

5. $d = \sqrt{(x_2 - x_1)^2 + (y_2 - y_1)^2}$

   The formula above gives the distance, d, between two points (x_1, y_1) and (x_2, y_2). What is the distance between the two points $(2, -6)$ and $(-3, 4)$?

Quiz 70 $\cdots\cdots\cdots\cdots\cdots\cdots\cdots\cdots\cdots\cdots\cdots\cdots\cdots\cdots\cdots\cdots\cdots\cdots\cdots\cdots\cdots\cdots\cdots\cdots\cdots\cdots\cdots$

Simplify.

1. $\sqrt{9} - \sqrt[4]{16} \times \sqrt[5]{-32} - \sqrt[3]{-1}$

2. $\sqrt{27x^5y^2}$

3. $\dfrac{4}{\sqrt{2}} + \sqrt{5} \cdot \sqrt{10}$

Solve.

4. $\sqrt{x + 3} = \sqrt{2x - 7}$

5. The area of a square is 36 cm^2. What is the length of the diagonal of the square in simplest radical form?

Quiz 71 ··

Evaluate. Write your answers without exponents.

1. 3^{-2}

2. $(-4)^0$

3. $5^{-3} \cdot 5^5$

4. $2^{-1} \cdot 6^3 \cdot 6^{-2}$

5. $10^5 \cdot 2^{-3} \cdot (-5)^{-4}$

Quiz 72 ···

Simplify. Write your answers with positive exponents.

1. $4x^3x^2$

2. $3x^5 \cdot 2x^{-4}$

3. $x^2 \cdot 5x^{-5} \cdot 4x$

4. $\dfrac{x^5x^{-1}}{x^2}$

5. $\dfrac{x^3 \cdot 8x^{-4}}{-2x^2}$

Quiz 73 ···

Simplify. Write your answers with positive exponents.

1. $(2x^2)^5$

2. $(-3x^{-3})^2$

3. $(4x^{-4})^{-3}$

4. $\left(\dfrac{-2}{x}\right)^3$

5. $\left(\dfrac{3}{x^2}\right)^{-2}$

Quiz 74 ··

Simplify. Write your answers with positive exponents.

1. $x^0 \cdot (2x^2)^3$

2. $9x \cdot (-3x^5)^{-2}$

3. $(-6x^3)^2 \cdot (2x^{-3})^{-2}$

4. $\left(\dfrac{3x^4x^{-2}}{x^{-1}x^5} \right)^3$

5. $\dfrac{(-4x^2x^5)^3}{(8x^0x^7)^2}$

Quiz 75 ·· 85

Convert between scientific notation and standard form.

1. 240,000,000

2. 0.0000005

3. 4.9×10^{-4}

Simplify. Write your answers in scientific notation.

4. $(5 \times 10^5)(7 \times 10^7)$

5. $\dfrac{1.5 \times 10^5}{6 \times 10^8}$

Quiz 76

Convert between exponential form and radical form.

1. $\sqrt[3]{x^2}$

2. $x^{5/4}$

Evaluate. Write your answers without exponents. Do not use a calculator.

3. $9^{1/2}$

4. $16^{5/4}$

5. $1000^{-2/3}$

Quiz 77 ···

Simplify. Write your answers in exponential form with positive exponents.

1. $x^{1/2} \cdot x^{2/3}$

2. $\left(8x^{1/4}\right)^{4/3}$

3. $\left(\dfrac{27x^{5/4}}{x^{1/2}}\right)^{2/3}$

Simplify. Write your answers in radical form.

4. $\sqrt{x} \cdot \sqrt[3]{x}$

5. $\dfrac{\sqrt[6]{x^5}}{\sqrt[3]{x}}$

Quiz 78 ···

1. Which function models exponential growth?

   A) $y = 4x^2$ B) $y = 3(4)^x$

   C) $y = 2(0.9)^x$ D) $y = 5(1/4)^x$

2. Which function models exponential decay?

   A) $y = x^{-3}$ B) $y = 0.1(2)^x$

   C) $y = 0.3^x$ D) $y = 3(1.4)^x$

3. $y = 4\left(\frac{1}{5}\right)^x$

   What is the shape of the graph of the function above?

   A) 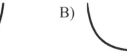   B)   C)   D)

Solve. Use a calculator if necessary. Round your answers to the nearest hundredth.

4. A pound of beef costs $6, and its price is increasing at a rate of 3% per year. How much will a pound of beef cost after 5 years?

5. A new car costs $18,000 and depreciates (decreases in value) at a rate of 15% per year. How much will the car be worth after 10 years?

Quiz 79 ···

Evaluate. Write your answers without exponents. Do not use a calculator.

1. $6^3 \cdot 3^{-2}$

2. $64^{2/3}$

Simplify. Write your answers in exponential form with positive exponents.

3. $4x^5 \cdot 3x^0 \cdot (6x^2)^{-1}$

4. $\left(1000x^{3/4}\right)^{1/3}$

Simplify. Write your answers in scientific notation.

5. $(5 \times 10^4)(6 \times 10^3)$

Quiz 80 ···

1. Which of the following is NOT a polynomial?

   A) 8 B) $x + x^{-2}$

   C) $x^2y^2 + 5$ D) $x^2 + 3x - 5$

2. $3x^4 - 5x^2 + x - 6$

   What is the degree and leading coefficient of the polynomial above?

Simplify. Write your answers in standard form.

3. $(2x + 7) - (4x - 2)$

4. $(-3x + 5) + (7x + x^2 - 5)$

5. $(x^3 + 4x + 9 - 2x^2) - (2 - 3x + x^2)$

Quiz 81 ···

Simplify. Write your answers in standard form.

1. $(-2x^4)(-5x^2)$

2. $3x^2(x^2 - 2x + 3)$

3. $(x + 4)(x + 3)$

4. $(x - 2)(5x + 1)$

5. $(2x + 1)(2x - 1)$

Quiz 82 ···

Simplify. Write your answers in standard form.

1. $(2x - 1)(x + 3)$

2. $(x + 4)(x^2 + 2x - 5)$

3. $(3x^2 - x + 4)(x + 2)$

4. $(x^2 + 2x - 3)(x^2 - x + 1)$

5. $(x + 2)(x - 1)(4x + 1)$

Quiz 83 ···

Simplify. Write your answers in standard form.

1. $(x + 3)^2$

2. $(3x - 2)^2$

3. $(2x + 5)(2x - 5)$

Use special product patterns to find the product. Do not use a calculator.

4. 43^2

5. 28×32

Quiz 84 ··

Simplify. Write your answers in standard form.

1. $(x + 2)(x - 3)$

2. $(x - 3)^2$

3. $(3x + 4)(3x - 4)$

4. $(2x + 5)^2$

5. $(x - 4)(4x + 3)$

Quiz 85 ···

Simplify. Write your answers in standard form.

1. $(25x^4) \div (-5x^3)$

2. $(6x^3 - 12x^2 + 9x) \div (3x)$

3. $(x^2 - 5x + 6) \div (x - 3)$

4. $(3x^2 - 11x - 4) \div (3x + 1)$

5. $(8x^2 + 6x - 5) \div (2x - 1)$

Quiz 86 ···

Simplify. Write your answers in standard form.

1. $(x^2 + 4x + 5) \div (x + 2)$

2. $(x^2 - 5x + 4) \div (x - 3)$

3. $(9x^2 - 6x + 4) \div (3x - 1)$

4. $(4x^2 + 1) \div (2x + 3)$

5. $(9x^2 - 5) \div (3x + 1)$

Quiz 87 ···

Simplify. Write your answers in standard form.

1. $(5x^2 - 2x + 3) - (3x^2 + x - 1)$

2. $(x + 3)(2x - 1)$

3. $(x - 2)^2$

4. $(2x^2 - 9x - 5) \div (x - 5)$

5. $(x^2 - 8x + 9) \div (x - 6)$

Quiz 93 ⸺⸺⸺⸺⸺⸺⸺⸺⸺⸺⸺⸺⸺⸺⸺⸺⸺⸺

Factor out the GCF.

1. $3x - 9$

2. $12x^2 + 16x$

3. $7x^2y^2 - 2x^2y$

4. $15x^5 + 12x^3 - 9x^2$

5. $x^3y^3 + 6x^2y^2 - 10xy$

Quiz 94 •••

Factor by grouping.

1. $x^3 - 3x^2 + 2x - 6$

2. $2x^3 + 8x^2 + 3x + 12$

3. $6x^5 - 10x^3 - 3x^2 + 5$

Factor out the GCF first, then factor by grouping.

4. $2x^3 + 2x^2 + 6x + 6$

5. $5x^5 - x^4 - 10x^3 + 2x^2$

Quiz 95 ···

Factor.

1. $x^2 + 5x + 6$

2. $x^2 - 4x + 3$

3. $x^2 + 2x - 8$

4. $x^2 + 7x + 10$

5. $x^2 + 3x - 28$

Quiz 96 ···

Factor.

1. $x^2 + 10x + 24$

2. $x^2 - 6x - 16$

Factor out the GCF first, then factor further.

3. $2x^2 - 4x - 30$

4. $4x^2 + 20x - 24$

5. $3x^2 - 27x + 42$

Quiz 97 ⋯⋯⋯⋯⋯⋯⋯⋯⋯⋯⋯⋯⋯⋯⋯⋯⋯⋯⋯⋯⋯⋯⋯⋯⋯⋯⋯⋯⋯⋯⋯⋯⋯⋯⋯⋯⋯

Factor.

1. $2x^2 + 3x + 1$

2. $8x^2 - 14x + 3$

3. $3x^2 - 10x - 8$

4. $5x^2 + 12x - 9$

5. $9x^2 - 24x + 16$

Quiz 98 ··

Factor.

1. $6x^2 - 5x - 6$

2. $3x^2 - 11x - 4$

3. $4x^2 + 16x + 7$

4. $5x^2 + 19x + 12$

5. $12x^2 - 17x - 5$

Quiz 99 ···

Factor.

1. $x^2 + 6x + 9$

2. $x^2 - 36$

3. $x^2 - 14x + 49$

4. $9x^2 - 4$

5. $4x^2 + 20x + 25$

Quiz 100 ···

Factor completely.

1. $x^2 + 5x - 14$

2. $2x^2 - 3x - 9$

3. $5x^2 - 10x + 5$

4. $-4x^2 + 49$

5. $-3x^2 + 6x + 45$

Quiz 101 ··

Factor completely.

1. $-6x^2 - 9x + 60$

2. $x^4 - 16$

3. $20x^2 + 11x - 3$

4. $5x^3 + 20x^2 + 20x$

5. $2x^3 + 4x^2 - 32x - 64$

Quiz 102 ···

Factor completely.

1. $x^2 + 7x + 10$

2. $12x^2 - 5x - 3$

3. $-2x^3 + 50x$

4. $4x^3 + x^2 - 16x - 4$

5. $9x^4 + 6x^3 + x^2$

Quiz 103 ··

Solve by taking square roots. Leave your answers as improper fractions or radicals in simplest form, if applicable.

1. $x^2 = 75$

2. $3x^2 = 48$

3. $x^2 - 24 = 0$

4. $4x^2 - 121 = 0$

5. $32 - 3x^2 = 17$

Quiz 104 ···

Solve by taking square roots. Leave your answers as improper fractions or radicals in simplest form, if applicable.

1. $5x^2 - 100 = 0$

2. $(x + 2)^2 = 81$

3. $(x - 5)^2 - 5 = 49$

4. $9(x - 1)^2 = 36$

5. $3(x + 4)^2 - 13 = 20$

Quiz 105 ···

Solve by factoring. Reduce fractions but leave them improper.

1. $x^2 + 7x + 10 = 0$

2. $x^2 - 25 = 0$

3. $x^2 - 24 = 2x$

4. $x^2 + 4x = 45$

5. $x^2 + 5x = 6x + 6$

Quiz 106 ···

Solve by factoring. Reduce fractions but leave them improper.

1. $4x^2 + x - 3 = 0$

2. $9x^2 - 4 = 0$

3. $2x^2 + 18 = 12x$

4. $x^2 + 4x + 4 = 9$

5. $2x^2 - 2x + 5 = x^2 + 5x - 7$

Quiz 107 ···

Solve by completing the square. Leave your answers as improper fractions or radicals in simplest form, if applicable.

1. $x^2 + 2x = 2$

2. $x^2 - 6x = 3$

3. $x^2 + 10x + 5 = 0$

4. $x^2 - 4x + 1 = 0$

5. $x^2 + 7x = 5x + 3$

Quiz 108 ···

Solve by completing the square. Leave your answers as improper fractions or radicals in simplest form, if applicable.

1. $x^2 + 4x = 1$

2. $3x^2 + 4x = 4$

3. $2x^2 + 12x - 10 = 0$

4. $5x^2 - 6x - 11 = 0$

5. $4x^2 = x^2 + 12x - 3$

Quiz 109 ···

Solve by the quadratic formula. Leave your answers as improper fractions or radicals in simplest form, if applicable.

1. $x^2 - 8 = 0$

2. $x^2 + 4x + 3 = 0$

3. $2x^2 - 7x + 4 = 0$

4. $5x^2 + 2x - 1 = 0$

5. $9x^2 - 12x + 4 = 0$

Quiz 110 ··

Solve by the quadratic formula. Leave your answers as improper fractions or radicals in simplest form, if applicable.

1. $4x^2 - 8x + 3 = 0$

2. $6x^2 - 54 = 0$

3. $x^2 - 5x = 3x - 5$

4. $5x^2 + 11x = x - 4$

5. $3x^2 - 7x = x^2 - 2$

Quiz 111 ··

Solve using any method. Leave your answers as improper fractions or radicals in simplest form, if applicable.

1. $(x - 3)^2 - 25 = 0$

2. $x^2 + 3x - 10 = 0$

3. $2x^2 + 4x - 8 = 0$

4. $x^2 + 5x + 3 = 0$

5. $3x^2 + 6x + 2 = 0$

Quiz 112 ···

Find the discriminant and state the number of solutions.

1. $x^2 - 6x + 9 = 0$

2. $x^2 - 5x + 7 = 0$

3. $2x^2 + 5x - 2 = 0$

Solve using any method. Leave your answers as improper fractions or radicals in simplest form, if applicable.

4. $x^2 - 8x + 5 = 0$

5. $2x^2 - 7x - 4 = 0$

Quiz 113 ··

1. The sum of two positive integers is 9. The sum of their squares is 53. Find the integers.

2. The difference between two positive integers is 4. The sum of the larger and the square of the smaller is 24. Find the integers.

3. An isosceles right triangle has a hypotenuse of 2 feet. Find the perimeter of the triangle. Leave your answer in simplest radical form.

4. A rectangle has a width of 8 cm and a height of 7 cm. A strip of uniform width is cut around the rectangle to decrease its area by 36 cm^2. What is the width of the strip?

5. Two cars left an intersection at the same time. Car A traveled north and car B traveled east. When car A was 14 miles farther than car B from the intersection, the distance between the two cars was 16 miles more than car B had traveled. How far apart were they?

Quiz 114

Solve using any method. Leave your answers as improper fractions or radicals in simplest form, if applicable.

1. $2(x + 4)^2 - 16 = 0$

2. $x^2 + 10x + 24 = 0$

3. $5x^2 - 20x + 20 = 0$

4. $2x^2 + x - 2 = 0$

5. One leg of a right triangle is 4 cm longer than the shorter leg and 4 cm shorter than the hypotenuse. Find the dimensions of the triangle.

Quiz 115 ··

Graph by plotting the points for the given x-values.

1. $y = x^2 - 1$ for $x = -2, -1, 0, 1, 2$

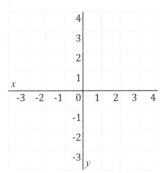

2. $y = -x^2 + 3$ for $x = -2, -1, 0, 1, 2$

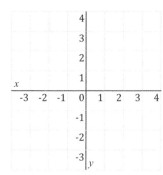

3. $y = x^2 - 2x$ for $x = -1, 0, 1, 2, 3$

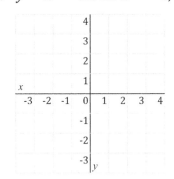

4. $y = \frac{1}{4}x^2 - 2$ for for $x = -4, -2, 0, 2, 4$

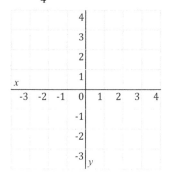

5. $y = -2x^2 + 4x + 2$ for $x = -1, 0, 1, 2, 3$

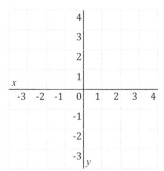

Quiz 116 ···

Find the vertex.

1. $y = x^2 + 8x + 9$

2. $y = -x^2 + 6x - 1$

Graph by plotting the vertex and two additional points on each side of the vertex. Use the y-intercept when possible.

3. $y = x^2 + 2x - 3$

4. $y = x^2 - 4x + 4$

5. $y = -\frac{1}{2}x^2 + 2x$

Quiz 117 ···

Find the vertex.

1. $y = 4(x - 5)^2 + 3$

2. $y = -(x + 2)^2 - 9$

Graph by plotting the vertex and one additional point on each side of the vertex. Use the y-intercept when possible.

3. $y = (x - 2)^2 - 3$

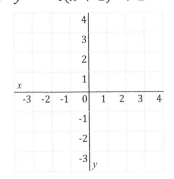

4. $y = -4(x + 1)^2 + 2$

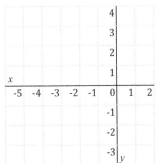

5. $y = \frac{1}{4}(x + 2)^2 - 1$

Quiz 118 ··

Find the vertex.

1. $y = (x + 3)(x - 3)$

2. $y = -\frac{2}{3}(x - 3)(x - 9)$

Graph by plotting the vertex and x-intercepts.

3. $y = -(x - 1)(x - 3)$

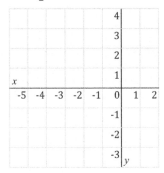

4. $y = \frac{1}{2}x(x + 4)$

5. $y = 2(x + 1)(x - 1)$

Quiz 119 ···

Convert to vertex form.

1. $y = x^2 + 6x + 5$

2. $y = -2x^2 + 8x - 1$

Convert to intercept form.

3. $y = x^2 - 2x - 8$

4. $y = \frac{1}{2}x^2 + 3x$

Graph.

5. $y = x^2 - 2x - 3$

Quiz 120 ···

Find the vertex, y-intercept, and x-intercepts (if any).

1. $y = -4(x - 1)^2$

2. $y = \frac{1}{3}(x + 1)(x - 5)$

3. $y = -x^2 - 4x + 5$

4. $y = 2x^2 - 8$

5. $y = -x^2 + 6x - 5$

Quiz 121 ···

Find an equation of each parabola in standard form.

1.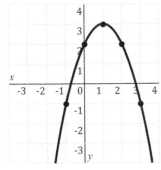

2. A parabola has a vertex at $(5, 3)$ and passes through $(2, -6)$.

3. A parabola has a vertex at $(-3, 0)$ and passes through $(-1, 8)$.

4. A parabola has zeros at -2 and 1 and passes through the point $(0, -6)$.

5. A parabola has zeros at 0 and 8 and passes through the point $(-2, 5)$.

Quiz 122 ···

Find an equation of each transformed parabola in vertex form.

1. The parabola $y = x^2$ is shifted right 3 units.

2. The parabola $y = x^2$ is flipped over the x-axis and shifted up 2 units.

3. The parabola $y = x^2$ is shifted left 2 units and down 5 units.

4. The parabola $y = x^2$ is scaled by 3 and shifted right 4 units and up 2 units.

5. The parabola $y = x^2$ is scaled by 2, flipped over the x-axis, and shifted left 1 unit.

Quiz 123 ···

1. $h(t) = -16t^2 + 128t$

    A ball is shot vertically upward from ground level with an initial speed of 128 feet per second. The function above models its height h, in feet, after t seconds. When does the ball reach its maximum height?

2. $h(t) = -16t^2 + 144$

    A ball is dropped from a height of 144 feet. The function above models its height h, in feet, after t seconds. When will the ball hit the ground?

3. $h(t) = -16t^2 + 64t + 80$

    A ball is thrown straight up from a height of 80 feet with an initial speed of 64 feet per second. The function above models its height h, in feet, after t seconds. When will the ball be at a height of 80 feet again?

4. $h(t) = -16t^2 + 32t + 240$

    A ball is thrown straight up from a height of 240 feet with an initial speed of 32 feet per second. The function above models its height h, in feet, after t seconds. What is the maximum height reached by the ball?

5. $c(x) = 0.2x^2 - 8x + 90$

    The cost for producing a certain part is modeled by the function above, where x is the number of parts produced a day. For what number of parts is the cost minimized? (*Hint*: Find the x-value of the vertex of the parabola.)

Quiz 124 ···

Convert to vertex form, then graph.

1. $y = x^2 - 2x + 2$

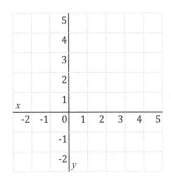

2. $y = -\frac{1}{2}x^2 + 4x - 6$

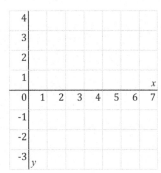

3. A parabola has zeros at 2 and 6 and passes through the point $(7, -5)$. What is the vertex of the parabola?

4. The parabola $y = x^2$ is scaled by 3, flipped over the x-axis, and shifted 4 units up. Find an equation of the transformed parabola in vertex form.

5. $h(t) = -16t^2 + 96t + 256$

   A ball is thrown straight up from a height of 256 feet with an initial speed of 96 feet per second. The function above models its height h, in feet, after t seconds. When does the ball reach its maximum height?

Quiz 125 ···

Simplify. State any excluded values.

1. $\dfrac{5x^3}{35x^2}$

2. $\dfrac{x^2 - 4}{x^2 + 2x}$

3. $\dfrac{x + 7}{x^2 + 5x - 14}$

4. $\dfrac{x^2 - 6x + 9}{2x^2 - 5x - 3}$

5. $\dfrac{x^3 + 5x^2 + 4x}{x^3 + 4x^2 - x - 4}$

Quiz 126 ··

Simplify. State any excluded values.

1. $\dfrac{7}{2x^2} \cdot \dfrac{4x}{21}$

2. $\dfrac{x^2 + 3x}{x + 5} \div \dfrac{x + 3}{2x + 10}$

3. $\dfrac{x^2 - 4x + 4}{3x^2 - 6x} \cdot \dfrac{x^2}{x - 2}$

4. $\dfrac{x^2 + 2x - 15}{2x^2 + 3x} \cdot \dfrac{2x + 3}{x + 5}$

5. $\dfrac{2x^2 - 3x - 20}{4x^3 - 25x} \div \dfrac{x^2 - 4x}{x^2}$

Quiz 127 ···

Simplify. State any excluded values.

1. $\dfrac{x^2 + 9}{x + 3} + \dfrac{6x}{x + 3}$

2. $\dfrac{x + 2}{x} - \dfrac{x + 5}{x + 3}$

3. $\dfrac{x}{x^2 - 4} - \dfrac{2}{x^2 - 4}$

4. $\dfrac{x + 2}{x - 3} - \dfrac{x - 2}{x^2 - 5x + 6}$

5. $\dfrac{3x + 9}{2x^2 + 7x + 3} + \dfrac{x}{2x + 1}$

Quiz 128 ···

Solve. Check for extraneous solutions.

1. $\dfrac{1}{2} - \dfrac{3}{x} = \dfrac{1}{2x}$

2. $\dfrac{2}{x+4} = \dfrac{3}{x+5}$

3. $\dfrac{x}{x+4} - \dfrac{1}{x} = \dfrac{1}{x}$

4. $\dfrac{x}{x+3} = \dfrac{1}{x} - \dfrac{3}{x+3}$

5. $\dfrac{3}{x} - \dfrac{1}{x+2} = \dfrac{x-2}{x^2+2x}$

Quiz 129 ···

Solve. Check for extraneous solutions.

1. $\dfrac{x}{4} + \dfrac{3}{x} = \dfrac{x+2}{x}$

2. $\dfrac{1}{3x} - \dfrac{x+1}{2x^2} = \dfrac{x-4}{x^2}$

3. $\dfrac{x+1}{2x+3} = \dfrac{x}{2x+1}$

4. $\dfrac{x}{3x-1} + \dfrac{1}{x-1} = \dfrac{1}{3x-1}$

5. $\dfrac{x}{x-2} - \dfrac{2}{x+3} = \dfrac{10}{x^2+x-6}$

Quiz 130 ··

1. Pipe A can drain a pool in 3 hours. Pipe B can drain the pool in 6 hours. How long will it take to drain the pool when both pipes are used?

2. Lucas can mow the lawn by himself in 20 minutes. William can mow the lawn in 30 minutes. How long will it take to mow the lawn if they work together?

3. Mark and James can paint a fence together in 3 hours. James alone can paint the fence in 5 hours. How long will it take Mark to paint the fence alone?

4. Sam can complete a certain task in 2 hours. Ella can do it in 3 hours, and Adam can do it in 6 hours. How long will it take to complete the task if they work together?

5. Pipe A can fill a pool four times faster than pipe B. When both pipes are open, they fill the pool in 4 hours. How long will it take pipe A to fill the pool alone?

Quiz 131 ···

Simplify. State any excluded values.

1. $\dfrac{x^3 + 3x^2 - 10x}{x^3 + 5x^2 - 4x - 20}$

2. $\dfrac{x^2 - 4x - 12}{3x + 4} \div \dfrac{x + 2}{3x^2 + 4x}$

3. $\dfrac{x^2 - 11}{x^2 - 3x - 10} - \dfrac{2}{x - 5}$

Solve. Check for extraneous solutions.

4. $\dfrac{1}{x} - \dfrac{x}{x + 4} = \dfrac{4}{x^2 + 4x}$

5. Machine A can do a certain job in 9 hours. Machine B can do the same job in 6 hours. How long will it take to do the job if both machines are used?

Quiz 138 ··

Find the mean, median, and mode. Use a calculator if necessary.

1. 3, 5, 9, 3, 6, 2, 7

2. 2, 8, 3, 6, 9, 7, 9, 4

3. 30, 15, 20, 15, 18, 10

Find the value of x.

4. 4, 5, 9, x, 2, 8; mean = 6

5. 3, x, 6, 2, 7, 3, 9; mean = 5

Quiz 139 ··

Find the range and standard deviation. Use a calculator if necessary. Round your answers to the nearest tenth.

1. 3, 3, 2, 8

2. 7, 4, 5, 5, 4

3. 3, 3, 3, 3, 3, 3

4. 2, 5, 1, 6, 4, 7, 3

5. 4, 5, 4, 3, 6, 8

Quiz 140 ··

Find the five-number summary.

1. 8, 3, 4, 9, 2, 8

2. 2, 7, 4, 8, 4, 6, 6, 4

The box-and-whisker plot shows the scores of a class on an algebra test. Answer the questions.

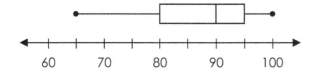

3. What is the median score?

4. What is the range of the scores?

5. What percentage of the class scored between 80 and 90?

Quiz 141

1. Find the median in the stem-and-leaf plot.

Stem	Leaf
0	7, 9
1	0, 0, 5, 7, 8
2	3, 3, 7, 9

2. The frequency table shows the favorite crayon color names from a survey of children. How many children were surveyed?

Color name	Frequency
Pink Flamingo	7
Inchworm	9
Outer Space	4

3. The dot plot shows the number of goals a soccer team scored at each game this season. During how many games did the team score 5 or more goals?

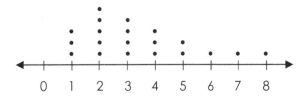

4. In the dot plot above, what is the median number of goals scored by the team?

5. The histogram shows the ages of children who visited a city fair on a certain day. How many children visited the fair?

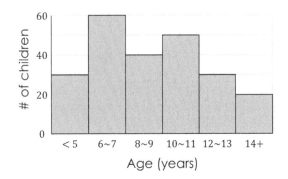

Quiz 142 ··

Describe the shape of each distribution.

1.

2.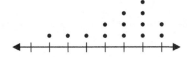

3.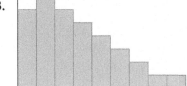

Use the graphs above to answer the question.

4. What is the better measure of central tendency for the box-and-whisker plot above, median or mean?

5. What is the better measure of variability for the dot plot above, standard deviation or interquartile range?

Quiz 143 ···

Identify the type of correlation.

1. Height and weight of a large group of people

2. Temperature and elevation

3.

4.

5. Which equation best describes the line of best fit for the first plot above?

   A) $y = x$

   B) $y = x + 5$

   C) $y = -x$

   D) $y = -x + 5$

Quiz 144 ···

A restaurant surveyed its customers about their preference. Answer the questions.

	Steak	Pasta
Soup	52	46
Salad	48	54

1. How many customers participated in the survey?

2. How many customers in the survey prefer pasta?

3. What percentage of the customers prefer steak with soup?

4. What percentage of the customers prefer pasta with salad?

5. Among the customers who prefer steak, what percentage prefer soup?

Quiz 145 ···

1. Find the mean, median, and mode of the data set {2, 6, 5, 6, 8, 3}.

2. What is the median and interquartile range of the data?

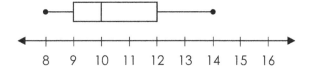

3. Describe the shape of the distribution shown in the plot above.

4. What are the appropriate measures of center and variation for the distribution above?

   A) Mean and standard deviation

   B) Mean and interquartile range

   C) Median and standard deviation

   D) Median and interquartile range

5. The table comes from a survey of students. What percentage of the students are female students with no pet?

	Pet(s)	No pet
Male	40	80
Female	32	48

Quiz 146

Write the probability as a simplified fraction.

1. A ball is randomly drawn from a bag containing 5 white, 10 black, and 5 grey balls. What is the probability that the ball is white?

2. A die is rolled. What is the probability of getting a single-digit number?

3. A spinner with 10 equal sections marked 1 through 10 is spun. What is the probability of landing on a multiple of 3?

4. Logan hit a baseball on 14 out of 30 tries during practice. What is the experimental probability that he will hit the ball on his next try?

5. Luke shot 27 free throws and made 18 of them. What is the experimental probability that he misses the next free throw?

Quiz 147 ···

Find the total number of possible outcomes.

1. You spin a spinner with eight equal sections numbered 1 through 8.

2. You select a day from a non-leap year. (A leap year has 366 days.)

3. You toss a coin and select a letter from the alphabet.

4. You buy a combo meal that consists of 1 sandwich, 1 side, and 1 drink. You have 5 choices of sandwiches, 6 choices of sides, and 2 choices of drinks.

5. You roll a die and spin a spinner with four equal sections marked 1 through 4.

Quiz 148 ···

Find the total number of possible outcomes.

1. You toss a coin four times.

2. You roll a die and toss two coins.

3. You answer 3 multiple-choice questions with 4 options for each.

4. You make a 3-digit number using the digits 1 to 5 with repetition of digits.

5. You make a 3-digit number using the digits 1 to 5 without repetition of digits.

Quiz 149 ···

Write the probability as a simplified fraction.

1. A coin is tossed twice. What is the probability of getting heads both times?

2. A die is rolled twice. What is the probability of getting a 5 on the first roll and an odd number on the second roll?

3. A die is rolled twice. What is the probability of getting a number greater than 4 on both rolls?

4. A spinner with five equal sections marked 1 through 5 is spun twice. What is the probability of getting an odd number on the first spin and an even number on the second spin?

5. A bag contains 2 yellow, 4 pink, and 4 white balls. Two balls are drawn at random with replacement (putting the ball drawn back in the bag before drawing the next ball). What is the probability of drawing two yellow balls?

Quiz 150 ··

Write the probability as a simplified fraction.

1. Two cards are randomly selected from a stack of five cards numbered 1 to 5, without replacement. What is the probability of selecting two odd numbers?

2. A bag contains 3 red and 7 white balls. Two balls are drawn at random without replacement. What is the probability of drawing two red balls?

3. A 2-digit number is formed using the digits 1 through 9 with repetition not allowed. What is the probability that the number is 55?

4. A spinner with five equal sections marked 1 through 5 is spun twice. What is the probability of getting the same number on both spins?

5. A die is rolled twice. What is the probability of getting a sum equal to 9?

Quiz 151 ···

Write the probability as a simplified fraction.

1. A die is rolled. What is the probability of rolling a 2 or an odd number?

2. A die is rolled. What is the probability of rolling a 2 or a prime number?

3. A die is rolled. What is the probability of rolling a number greater than 3 or an odd number?

4. A card is randomly drawn from a standard deck of 52 cards. What is the probability of drawing an ace or face card?

5. A card is randomly drawn from a standard deck of 52 cards. What is the probability of drawing a black or face card?

Quiz 152 ···

Solve. Use a calculator if necessary. Assume repetition is not allowed.

1. In how many different ways can you arrange the letters of the word LIGHT?

2. How many different committees of 3 people can be formed from a group of 5?

3. In how many different ways can 1st-, 2nd-, and 3rd-place prizes be awarded to 10 students?

4. How many different 3-digit numbers can you make using only odd digits?

5. In how many different ways can 2 cards be drawn simultaneously from a standard deck of 52 cards?

Quiz 153 ···

Solve. Use a calculator if necessary. Assume repetition is not allowed.

1. In how many different ways can you choose 3 toppings from 8 available toppings for your pizza?

2. In how many different ways can you arrange the letters of the word SNOW?

3. In how many different ways can you arrange the letters of the word FORMULA taking 3 letters at a time?

4. How many different teams of 4 players can be formed from 9 players?

5. In how many different ways can you draw the names of 2 raffle winners from a basket of 20 names if both winners get the same prize?

Quiz 154 ···

The letters of the word **BEGIN** are rearranged in a random order. Write the probability as a simplified fraction.

1. What is the probability that an arrangement spells BEING?

2. What is the probability that an arrangement begins with a vowel?

3. What is the probability that an arrangement begins and ends with a vowel?

Two balls are drawn simultaneously from a bag containing 4 yellow, 2 pink, and 3 white balls. Write the probability as a simplified fraction.

4. What is the probability of drawing 2 yellow balls?

5. What is the probability of drawing no pink balls?

Quiz 155 ···

Write the probability as a simplified fraction.

1. A ball is randomly drawn from a bag containing 2 white, 3 black, and 5 grey balls. What is the probability that the ball is white?

2. A coin is tossed three times. What is the probability of getting tails three times?

3. A die is rolled twice. What is the probability of getting the same number twice?

4. A die is rolled. What is the probability of rolling a prime number or an odd number?

5. Five cards numbered 1 through 5 are randomly arranged. What is the probability that a card with an even number comes first?

Quiz 158 ···

Solve.

1. $7x - 8 = 3(x + 5) - 7$

2. $4|x - 5| - 9 = 15$

3. $-23 < 7 - 5x \leq 42$

4. $3 + |-6x| \geq 21$

5. The sum of three even consecutive integers is 78. Find the integers.

Quiz 159 ··

Graph.

1. $x - 2y = 2$

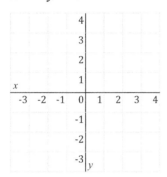

2. $y = |x - 1| - 2$

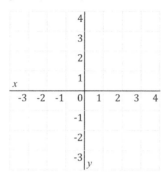

3. $3x + y > 3$

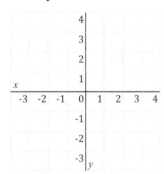

4. A line passes through $(-1, 7)$ and $(2, -5)$. Write an equation of the line in slope-intercept form.

5. A bike rental shop charges a flat fee of $5 plus $7 per hour for renting a bike. Which expression represents the rental cost?

A) $5x + 7$, where x is the number of hours

B) $7x + 5$, where x is the number of hours

C) $5x + 7$, where x is the number of bikes

D) $7x + 5$, where x is the number of bikes

Quiz 160 ···

Solve.

1. $y = -2x - 9$
    $4x + 5y = 3$

2. $2x + 3y = 8$
    $5x - 3y = -1$

3. $3x + 2y = 7$
    $5x + 4y = 15$

4. Flying with the wind, an airplane can fly 1,680 miles in 6 hours. Flying against the wind, the plane can fly the same distance in 7 hours. Find the speed of the plane in still air and the speed of the wind.

Graph the solution set.

5. $x \geq 0$ and $x + 3y < 3$

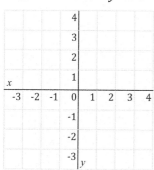

Quiz 161 ···

Us Use the graph of f to answer the question.

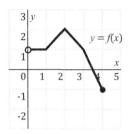

1. Find the domain and range of $f(x)$.

2. $f(2) + f^{-1}(-1) = ?$

Solve.

3. Is the table linear, quadratic, or exponential?

x	0	1	2	3	4
y	9	5	1	−3	−7

4. Suppose y varies inversely with x, and $y = 2$ when $x = 8$. Find x when $y = 4$.

5. Write the explicit formula of the sequence 5, 8, 11, 14, 17, ...

Quiz 162 ⋯⋯⋯⋯⋯⋯⋯⋯⋯⋯⋯⋯⋯⋯⋯⋯⋯⋯⋯⋯⋯⋯⋯⋯

Simplify.

1. $\sqrt{81} \div \sqrt[4]{81} - \sqrt[3]{8} \times \sqrt[5]{-1}$

2. $\sqrt{80x^2yz^2}$

3. $3\sqrt{24} - \sqrt{3}\left(\sqrt{6} + 2\sqrt{18}\right) + \sqrt{32}$

Solve.

4. $\sqrt{2x+5} = \sqrt{x+9}$

5. The diagonal of a rectangle is 14 inches. Its width is 7 inches. What is the length of the rectangle in simplest radical form?

Quiz 163 ···

Simplify. Write your answers in exponential form with positive exponents.

1. $3x^4 \cdot 5x^{-3}$

2. $x^5 \cdot (2x^2)^{-2}$

3. $(27x^3)^{2/3}$

4. $\left(\dfrac{32x^{1/2}}{x^{1/4}}\right)^{4/5}$

Write an exponential function that models the situation, then solve. Use a calculator.

5. A rare coin costs \$200 and appreciates (increases in value) at a rate of 5% per year. How much will the coin be worth after 5 years? Round to the nearest hundredth.

Quiz 164

Simplify in standard form. Use long division.

1. $(x - 4)(x + 4)(x - 2)$

2. $(3x^2 + 2x - 8) \div (x + 2)$

Factor completely.

3. $3x^2 + 10x + 3$

4. $8x^3 - 16x^2 + 8x$

5. $-4x^3 - 12x^2 + x + 3$

Quiz 165

Solve using any method. Leave your answers as improper fractions or radicals in simplest form, if applicable.

1. $2(x-1)^2 - 18 = 0$

2. $3x^2 - 9x + 6 = 0$

3. $x^2 + 6x + 3 = 0$

4. $4x^2 + 7x + 2 = 0$

5. A rectangle has an area of 90 cm². Its length is 3 cm longer than twice its width. Find the dimensions of the rectangle.

Quiz 166 ···

Find the vertex and intercepts, then graph.

1. $y = 2x^2 - 4x$

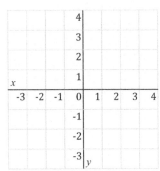

2. $y = -x^2 - 2x + 3$

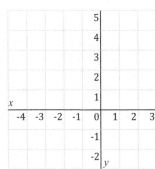

3. A parabola has a vertex at $(-2, -8)$ and passes through $(1, 10)$. What are the zeros of the parabola?

4. The parabola $y = x^2$ is scaled by 4, flipped over the x-axis, and shifted 5 units to the left. Find an equation of the transformed parabola in standard form.

5. $h(t) = -16t^2 + 96t$

A ball is shot vertically upward from ground level with an initial speed of 96 feet per second. The function above models its height h, in feet, after t seconds. When will the ball hit the ground?

Quiz 167 ···

Simplify. State any excluded values.

1. $\dfrac{4x^2 - 9}{2x^2 + 5x - 12}$

2. $\dfrac{5x + 15}{x^2 - 10x + 25} \div \dfrac{x + 3}{x - 5}$

3. $\dfrac{x}{x - 3} - \dfrac{x - 6}{x^2 - 7x + 12}$

Solve. Check for extraneous solutions.

4. $\dfrac{x}{x + 5} = \dfrac{4}{x} - \dfrac{3}{x + 5}$

5. Alex can clean the house in 1 hour. Working together, Alex and Leah can clean the house in just 15 minutes. How long will it take Leah alone to clean the house?

Quiz 168 ⋯⋯⋯⋯⋯⋯⋯⋯⋯⋯⋯⋯⋯⋯⋯⋯⋯⋯⋯⋯⋯⋯⋯⋯⋯⋯⋯⋯⋯⋯⋯

1. Find the mean, median, and mode of the data set {8, 13, 3, 8, 4, 1, 15, 6, 5, 7}.

2. What is the median of the data?

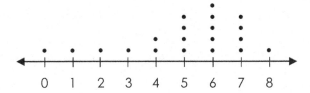

3. Describe the shape of the distribution shown in the plot above.

4. What type of correlation would you expect between the number of hours spent exercising and the amount of calories burned?

5. The table comes from a survey of students. What percentage of the surveyed female students have no pet?

	Pet(s)	No pet
Male	40	80
Female	32	48

Quiz 169 ···

Write the probability as a simplified fraction.

1. A spinner with five equal sections marked 1 through 5 is spun. What is the probability of landing on an odd number?

2. A die is rolled twice. What is the probability of getting a prime number on the first roll and an odd number on the second roll?

3. A die is rolled twice. What is the probability of getting a sum equal to 7?

4. A card is randomly drawn from a standard deck of 52 cards. What is the probability of drawing a red or face card?

5. Two balls are drawn simultaneously from a bag containing 2 yellow and 4 green balls. What is the probability of drawing 2 green balls?

Quiz 170 ···

Solve.

1. $5x + 12 = 7$

2. $3(x - 1) - x = 9 - 4x$

3. $0.4x + 1.7 = 2.02$

4. $\dfrac{1}{3}x + \dfrac{3}{4} = \dfrac{1}{2}x + \dfrac{1}{6}$

5. $4|3 - 2x| + 9 = 21$

Quiz 171 ···

Solve.

1. $9x - 2 \leq 34$

2. $6x - 4(2x + 1) > -8$

3. $-7 \leq 3 - 5x < 8$

4. $4x - 3 \geq 9$ or $6 - x < 8$

5. $\dfrac{2}{5}|x + 3| - 1 < \dfrac{3}{5}$

Quiz 172 ⋯⋯⋯⋯⋯⋯⋯⋯⋯⋯⋯⋯⋯⋯⋯⋯⋯⋯⋯⋯⋯⋯⋯ EP Math Algebra 1 Quizzes ⋯⋯⋯

Solve.

1. $y = x + 3$
   $3x + y = 15$

2. $2x + y = 7$
   $3x - y = -12$

3. $4x - y = -3$
   $8x - 2y = 9$

4. $2x + 7y = -4$
   $4x + 5y = 10$

5. $6x - 9y = 18$
   $4x - 6y = 12$

Quiz 173 ···

Solve. Check for extraneous solutions.

1. $4\sqrt{x} - 1 = 7$

2. $\sqrt{x - 3} + 5 = 2$

3. $\sqrt{2x - 1} - 3 = 0$

4. $\sqrt{3x + 8} = \sqrt{x + 4}$

5. $3\sqrt{x - 1} = \sqrt{6x - 7}$

Quiz 174 ···

Solve.

1. $x^2 - 3x - 18 = 0$

2. $(x - 1)^2 - 20 = 0$

3. $2x^2 + 4x + 7 = 0$

4. $4x^2 - 4x - 24 = 0$

5. $x^2 + 10x + 18 = 0$

Quiz 175 ···

Solve. Check for extraneous solutions.

1. $\dfrac{2}{4x-1} = \dfrac{3}{x+3}$

2. $\dfrac{2}{x} + \dfrac{x-3}{x+1} = \dfrac{1}{2}$

3. $\dfrac{x+2}{3x} - \dfrac{1}{x} = \dfrac{x-1}{9x}$

4. $\dfrac{x+1}{x+3} - \dfrac{1}{x-1} = \dfrac{4}{x+3}$

5. $\dfrac{x}{x+2} = \dfrac{x+16}{x^2-3x-10}$

Final Exam

Read the directions below carefully.

BEFORE THE TEST...

- Take 10 minutes to review your notes from Lessons 176 through 179.

- Get a calculator and blank sheets of paper for your calculations.

KEEP IN MIND...

- There are 40 questions on the test.

- Write your answers clearly in the space given. Do your work on separate paper.

- There is no time limit, but you must complete the test in ONE sitting.

- Do not use a calculator unless specifically stated that you may.

AFTER THE TEST...

- Grade yourself and record your score on your grading sheets.

- Calculate your final grade for the course. See your grading sheets for the details.

When you are ready,

begin the test.

1. $2x - 3 = -3x + 7$

   What is the value of x that satisfies the equation above?

2. If $f(x) = 2^x$, what is $f(3) - f(0)$?

3. What is the slope of the line that passes through $(2, 4)$ and $(-3, 1)$?

4. $\sqrt{3} \cdot \sqrt{12x^2}$

   If $x > 0$, simplify the expression above.

5. $(x + 3)(x - 3) + (x - 3)^2$

   Simplify the expression above in standard form.

6. Which equation is graphed below?

   A) $y = 3x$

   B) $x = 3y$

   C) $y = 3$

   D) $x = 3$

7. $|4x + 1| = 9$

   If a and b are the solutions to the equation above, what is the value of ab?

8. A line is perpendicular to $x + 3y = 6$ and passes through $(1, 5)$. Write an equation of the line in slope-intercept form.

9. $kx - 3y = 2$
   $5x + y = -1$

   What value of k makes the system of equations above have no solution?

10. $x^{-5}y^{-4} \cdot (2x^2y)^3$

    Simplify the expression above using positive exponents only.

11. Write an equation in vertex form for the parabola below.

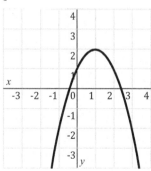

12. $|5 - 2x| \leq 11$

What is the solution set to the inequality above?

13. If $f(x) = x^2 - 8$ and $f(a) = 1$, what could be the values of a?

14. $4x^3 + 8x^2 - x - 2$

Factor the polynomial above completely.

15. $x^2 - 2x - 2 = 0$

If a and b are the solutions to the equation above, what is the value of $a + b$?

16. What is the value of $9^{1/2} + 8^{2/3} + 81^{1/4}$?

17. Write an equation in slope-intercept form for the line below.

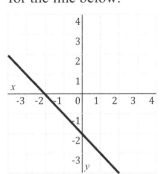

18. $2x + y = 5$
$x - 2y = 5$

What is the solution to the system of equations above? Write your answer as an ordered pair.

19. $4\sqrt{x + 1} - 2 = 6$

What is the solution to the equation above?

20. $\dfrac{x^2 - 2x + 1}{x^2 + 2x - 3}$

Simplify the expression above. Assume all denominators are nonzero.

21. The graph of $y = x^2 + 3x - 10$ has two x-intercepts. What is the distance between the x-intercepts?

22. Which equation is graphed below?

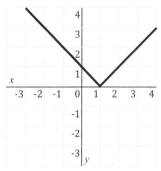

A) $y = |x - 1|$ B) $y = |x + 1|$

C) $y = |x| - 1$ D) $y = |x| + 1$

23. $\dfrac{1}{x+2} + \dfrac{2}{x-3} = \dfrac{1}{2}$

   What are the solutions to the equation above?

24. The height of an object varies directly with the length of its shadow. If a tree 8 feet tall casts a shadow 10 feet long, how long will be the shadow of a tree that is 12 feet tall?

25. Owen has $1.05 in dimes and nickels. He has 3 more dimes than nickels. How many coins of each type does he have?

26. Alex can complete a certain task in 10 hours. Working together, Alex and Eli can do it in 6 hours. How long will it take Eli alone to complete the task?

27. Write an inequality in slope-intercept form for the graph below.

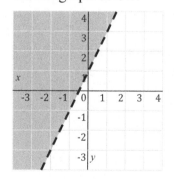

28. A water tank with 300 gallons of water is emptied using two pumps. One pump pumps water out at a rate of 11 gallons and the other at a rate of 9 gallons. Write an equation in slope-intercept form that represents the amount of water, y, in the tank after x minutes.

29. Two trains leave stations 250 miles apart at the same time and travel toward each other. One train travels at 60 mph while the other travels at 65 mph. How long will it take for the two trains to meet?

30. A restaurant has 20 tables that can seat a total of 90 people. Some tables seat 4 people and the others seat 6 people. How many tables seat 4 people? How many tables seat 6 people?

31. Which table does NOT represent a linear function?

A)

x	0	2	4	6	8
y	−7	−3	1	5	9

B)

x	−2	−1	0	1	2
y	3	4	5	6	7

C)

x	0	1	2	3	4
y	1	2	4	8	16

D)

x	−8	−4	0	4	8
y	9	7	5	3	1

32. A rectangle has a perimeter of 20 inches and an area of 24 square inches. Find the dimensions of the rectangle.

33. How many liters of a 25% saline solution must be mixed with 4 liters of a 40% saline solution to make a 30% saline solution?

34. A six-sided die is thrown three times. What is the probability of getting a prime number on all three rolls?

You may use a calculator for questions 35–40. Round your answers to the nearest whole number, if necessary.

35. 5, 12, 19, 26, 33, ...

What is the 15th term of the sequence above?

36. $h(t) = -16t^2 + 48t + 64$

A ball is thrown vertically upwards from the top of a building of height 64 feet with an initial speed of 48 feet per second. Its height h, in meters, after t seconds is given by the function above. How long will the ball be in the air before it hits the ground?

37. The hypotenuse of a right triangle is 17 cm, and one of its legs is 8 cm. What is the perimeter of the triangle?

38. During a science experiment, Lisa found that bacteria double every 20 minutes. There were 10 bacteria in the beginning. How many bacteria will be there after 3 hours?

39. A survey asked a group of teens and adults whether they prefer online shopping or in-store shopping. The table below shows the results of the survey. What percentage of the teens prefer online shopping?

	Online	In-store	Total
Teens	64	13	77
Adults	53	35	88
Total	117	48	165

40. Brian randomly arranged six textbooks on his shelf. What is the probability that math comes first? Write your answer as a fraction in simplest form.

STOP
This is the end of the test.
Review your answers before grading.

Answers

Note that the worked-out solutions do not restate the problems but rather show the subsequent steps.

Quiz 1

1. The first step is **C**.

2. $3 + 4 = 7$

3. $28 - 12 \div 3 = 28 - 4 = 24$

4. $5^2 - 4 \times (8 - 3) = 5^2 - 4 \times 5 = 25 - 20 = 5$

5. $(-3)^4 \div 9 \times (-1)^3 + 8 = 81 \div 9 \times (-1) + 8$
   $= 9 \times (-1) + 8 = -9 + 8 = -1$

Quiz 2

1. $4(-2) + 7 = -1$

2. $5^2 - 4 \cdot 5 \cdot 4 + 4 \cdot 4^2 = 9$

3. $(2x - x) + (-3 + 5) = x + 2$

4. $5x + 5 - 8 + 2x = (5x + 2x) + (5 - 8) = 7x - 3$

5. $x - 3x^2 + 3x + 5x + x^2$
   $= (-3x^2 + x^2) + (x + 3x + 5x) = -2x^2 + 9x$

Quiz 3

1. The first step is **A**.

2. Subtract 4 from both sides: $\quad x = 6$

3. Divide both sides by -7: $\quad x = -9$

4. Subtract 4 from both sides: $\quad 5x = 15$
   Divide both sides by 5: $\quad x = 3$

5. Subtract 9 from both sides: $\quad -3x = 15$
   Divide both sides by -3: $\quad x = -5$

Quiz 4

1. Subtract $7x$ from both sides: $\quad -5x + 1 = 3$
   Subtract 1 from both sides: $\quad -5x = 2$
   Divide both sides by -5: $\quad x = -2/5$

2. Simplify each side: $\quad 2x + 2 = -2x + 8$
   Add $2x$ to both sides: $\quad 4x + 2 = 8$
   Subtract 2 from both sides: $\quad 4x = 6$
   Divide both sides by 4: $\quad x = 6/4$
   Simplify: $\quad x = 3/2$

3. Simplify each side: $\quad 8 = -4x + 15$
   Switch sides: $\quad -4x + 15 = 8$
   Subtract 15 from both sides: $\quad -4x = -7$
   Divide both sides by -4: $\quad x = 7/4$

4. Simplify each side: $\quad 6x - 7 = 4x - 5$
   Subtract $4x$ from both sides: $\quad 2x - 7 = -5$
   Add 7 to both sides: $\quad 2x = 2$
   Divide both sides by 2: $\quad x = 1$

5. Simplify each side: $\quad -x - 4 = 2x - 6$
   Subtract $2x$ from both sides: $\quad -3x - 4 = -6$
   Add 4 to both sides: $\quad -3x = -2$
   Divide both sides by -3: $\quad x = 2/3$

Quiz 5

1. The least common denominator is 12.

2. Multiply both sides by 10: $\quad 3x - 12 = -5x + 4$
   Add $5x$ to both sides: $\quad 8x - 12 = 4$
   Add 12 to both sides: $\quad 8x = 16$
   Divide both sides by 8: $\quad x = 2$

3. Multiply both sides by 100: $\quad 2x + 25 = -3x - 50$
   Add $3x$ to both sides: $\quad 5x + 25 = -50$
   Subtract 25 from both sides: $\quad 5x = -75$
   Divide both sides by 5: $\quad x = -15$

4. Multiply both sides by 20: $\quad 15x + 4 = 10x + 8$
   Subtract $10x$ from both sides: $\quad 5x + 4 = 8$
   Subtract 4 from both sides: $\quad 5x = 4$
   Divide both sides by 5: $\quad x = 4/5$

5. Multiply both sides by 4: $\quad 2(3x + 1) = 8x + 3$
   Simplify each side: $\quad 6x + 2 = 8x + 3$
   Subtract $8x$ from both sides: $\quad -2x + 2 = 3$
   Subtract 2 from both sides: $\quad -2x = 1$
   Divide both sides by -2: $\quad x = -1/2$

Quiz 6

1. Write two equations: $\quad 3x = 21$ or $3x = -21$
   Solve each equation: $\quad x = 7$ or $x = -7$

2. Write two equations: $\quad x - 7 = 5$ or $x - 7 = -5$
   Solve each equation: $\quad x = 12$ or $x = 2$

3. Isolate the bars. $\quad |4x + 1| = 5$
   Write two equations: $4x + 1 = 5$ or $4x + 1 = -5$
   Solve each equation: $\quad 4x = 4$ or $4x = -6$
   $\quad x = 1$ or $x = -3/2$

4. Isolate the bars: $\quad -3|x - 2| = -5$
   $\quad |x - 2| = 5/3$
   Write two equations: $\quad x - 2 = 5/3$ or $x - 2 = -5/3$
   Solve each equation: $\quad x = 11/3$ or $x = 1/3$

5. Isolate the bars: $\quad 5|2x + 3| = 15$
   $\quad |2x + 3| = 3$
   Write two equations: $\quad 2x + 3 = 3$ or $2x + 3 = -3$
   Solve each equation: $\quad 2x = 0$ or $2x = -6$
   $\quad x = 0$ or $x = -3$

Quiz 7

1. $2x = 6$
   $x = 3$

2. $8x - 1 = 5$
   $8x = 6$
   $x = 6/8 = 3/4$

3. $5x + 4 = -2x + 5$
   $7x + 4 = 5$
   $7x = 1$
   $x = 1/7$

4. $3x + 4 = 18x - 6$
   $-15x + 4 = -6$
   $-15x = -10$
   $x = (-10)/(-15)$
   $x = 2/3$

5. $-5|2x - 3| = -25$
   $|2x - 3| = 5$
   $2x - 3 = 5$ or $2x - 3 = -5$
   $2x = 8$ or $2x = -2$
   $x = 4$ or $x = -1$

Quiz 8

1. $0x + 3 = 5$
   $0x = 2$
   No solution

2. $2x - 5 = x$
   $x - 5 = 0$
   $x = 5$

3. $11x + 8 = 11x + 8$
   $0x + 8 = 8$
   $0x = 0$
   Infinitely many solutions

4. $|4x - 7| = -6$
   No solution

5. $3|x + 4| = 15$
   $|x + 4| = 5$
   $x + 4 = 5$ or $x + 4 = -5$
   $x = 1$ or $x = -9$

Quiz 9

1. Let x = the first even integer
   $x + 2$ = the second even integer
   The sum is 54, so $x + (x + 2) = 54$.
   Solve for x, and you get $x = 26$.
   The numbers are 26 and 28.

2. Let x = the width of the rectangle
   $3x - 5$ = the length of the rectangle
   Perimeter = 2(length + width), so $2(x + 3x - 5) = 30$.
   Solve for x, and you get $x = 5$.
   The rectangle is 5 feet by 10 feet.

3. Let x = the number of nickels
   $x + 2$ = the number of quarters
   Total value = x nickels at \$0.05 each + $(x + 2)$ quarters at \$0.25 each, so $0.05x + 0.25(x + 2) = 1.40$.
   Solve for x, and you get $x = 3$.
   Joey has 3 nickels and 5 quarters.

4. Let x = the cost before the tip
   $0.2x$ = the tip
   The total cost = the cost before the tip + the tip, so $x + 0.2x = 60$.
   Solve for x, and you get $x = 50$.
   The cost of the meal before the tip was \$50.

5. Let x = Emma's age
   $x + 4$ = Michael's age
   $x - 5$ = Emma's age 5 years ago
   $(x + 4) - 5$ = Michael's age 5 years ago
   The sum was 20, so $x - 5 + (x + 4) - 5 = 20$.
   Solve for x, and you get $x = 13$.
   Emma is 13 years old. Michael is 17 years old.

Quiz 10

1. Let t = travel time in hours
   $D = rt$, so $195 = 65t$.
   Solve for t, and you get $t = 3$.
   It will take 3 hours.

2. Let t = travel time in hours
   $D = rt$, so $30 \times (20/60) = 40t$.
   Solve for t, and you get $t = 1/4$.
   It will take 1/4 hour, or 15 minutes.

3. Let t = time it will take to meet each other
   Total distance traveled in t hours = Eli's distance + Alex's distance = 12 miles, so $4t + 6t = 12$.
   Solve for t, and you get $t = 1.2$.
   It will take 1.2 hours, or 1 hour and 12 minutes.

4. Let t = time taken to walk the circle the first time
   $4.5 - t$ = time taken to walk the circle the second time
   Distance walked the first time = distance walked the second time, so $4t = 5(4.5 - t)$.
   Solve for t, and you get $t = 2.5$.
   It took 2.5 hours to walk the circle at 4 mph, so the trail is $4 \times 2.5 = 10$ miles long.

5. Let t = time it will take Lucas to overtake Olivia
   $1 + t$ = time Olivia will travel until Lucas overtakes her
   Lucas's distance in t hours = Olivia's distance in $(1 + t)$ hours, so $14t = 10(1 + t)$.
   Solve for t, and you get $t = 2.5$.
   It will take 2.5 hours, or 2 hours and 30 minutes.

Quiz 11

1. Amount of salt = 20% of 30 grams = 0.2 × 30 = 6
   There are 6 grams of salt in the solution.

2. Let w = amount of water to mix
   Substance = salt = 10 g
   Solution = salt + water = 10 + w g
   Concentration = 25% = 0.25
   Concentration × solution = substance,
   so 0.25(10 + w) = 10.
   Solve for w, and you get w = 30.
   You need to mix 30 grams of water.

3. Let x = ounces of 10% solution
   x + 6 = ounces of 12% solution
   Acid in 10% solution + acid in 15% solution = acid in 12% solution, so 0.1x + 0.15 × 6 = 0.12(x + 6).
   Solve for x, and you get x = 9.
   We need to add 9 ounces of 10% solution.

4. Cost of nuts at \$4 per pound = \$4 × 2 = \$8
   Cost of nuts at \$6 per pound = \$6 × 3 = \$18
   Cost of the mixture = \$8 + \$18 = \$26
   Amount of the mixture = 2 + 3 = 5 pounds
   Unit price = cost/quantity = 26/5 = 5.2.
   The mixture costs \$5.20 per pound.

5. Let x = pounds of peanuts
   x + 6 = pounds of the mixture
   Cost of peanuts + cost of cashews = cost of the mixture, so 3x + 5 × 6 = 4.5(x + 6).
   Solve for x, and you get x = 2.
   We need to mix 2 pounds of peanuts.

Quiz 12

1. Switch sides: $x - y = 2x - 1$
   Subtract x from both sides: $-y = x - 1$
   Divide both sides by −1: $y = -x + 1$

2. Simplify each side: $3x + 3y = 4y + 5$
   Subtract 4y from both sides: $3x - y = 5$
   Subtract 3x from both sides: $-y = -3x + 5$
   Divide both sides by −1: $y = 3x - 5$

3. Multiply both sides by 6: $2y + 5x = 6x - 4$
   Subtract 5x from both sides: $2y = x - 4$
   Divide both sides by 2: $y = \dfrac{1}{2}x - 2$

4. Switch sides: $2l + 2w = P$
   Subtract 2l from both sides: $2w = P - 2l$
   Divide both sides by 2: $w = \dfrac{P - 2l}{2}$

5. Switch sides: $\dfrac{9}{5}C + 32 = F$

   Subtract 32 from both sides: $\dfrac{9}{5}C = F - 32$

   Multiply both sides by 5/9: $C = \dfrac{5}{9}(F - 32)$

Quiz 13

1. $6 + (3 \times 8 - 16 \div 4) \div 5 = 6 + (24 - 4) \div 5$
   $= 6 + 20 \div 5 = 6 + 4 = 10$

2. $6x = 15$
   $x = 15/6$
   $x = 5/2$

3. $6x - 12 = 3x - 8$
   $3x - 12 = -8$
   $3x = 4$
   $x = 4/3$

4. $3|2x + 5| = 15$
   $|2x + 5| = 5$
   $2x + 5 = 5$ or $2x + 5 = -5$
   $2x = 0$ or $2x = -10$
   $x = 0$ or $x = -5$

5. Let t = time it will take to be 920 miles apart
   Train 1's distance + train 2's distance = 920,
   so 110t + 120t = 920.
   Solve for t, and you get t = 4.
   It will take 4 hours.

Quiz 14

1. The statement **C** is true.

2.
x	−2	0	2	4	6
y	−7	−3	1	5	9

3.
x	−4	−2	0	2	4
y	8	5	2	−1	−4

4.

5.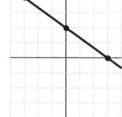

Quiz 15

1. You can pick any two points.
   Rise = 3 and run = –1, so slope = 3/(–1) = –3.
   (Or rise = –3 and run = 1, so slope = –3/1 = –3.)

2. $\dfrac{8-2}{1-(-2)} = \dfrac{6}{3} = 2$

3. $\dfrac{-2-10}{6-3} = \dfrac{-12}{3} = -4$

4. $\dfrac{0-4}{-8-2} = \dfrac{-4}{-10} = \dfrac{2}{5}$

5. $\dfrac{5-9}{-4-4} = \dfrac{-4}{-8} = \dfrac{1}{2}$

Quiz 16

1. $m = -1$, y-int = 5

2. $m = 1/4$, y-int = –3

3. $m = 1$, y-int = –2

4. $m = -2$, y-int = 3

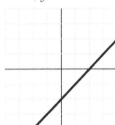

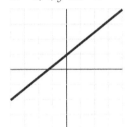

5. $m = 3/4$, y-int = 1

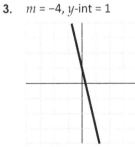

Quiz 17

1. $y = x - 5$

   $m = 1$, y-int = –5

2. $y = -\dfrac{1}{2}x + 4$

   $m = -1/2$, y-int = 4

3. $m = -4$, y-int = 1

4. $m = 1/3$, y-int = –1

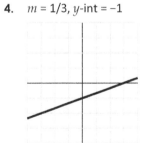

5. $m = 3/2$, y-int = 2

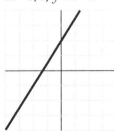

Quiz 18

1. When $y = 0$, $x = 6$.
   When $x = 0$, $y = -3$.
   x-int = 6, y-int = –3

2. When $y = 0$, $x = 3$.
   When $x = 0$, $y = 5$.
   x-int = 3, y-int = 5

3. x-int = 1, y-int = 3

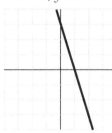

4. x-int = 3, y-int = –2

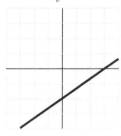

5. x-int = –3, y-int = –4

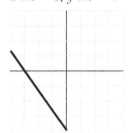

Quiz 19

1. $x = 3$

2. $y = -2$

3. 1st line: $m = 5$
   2nd line: $m = -1/5$
   Perpendicular

4. 1st line: $m = -3/4$
   2nd line: $m = -3$
   Neither

5. 1st line: $m = -2/3$
   2nd line: $m = -2/3$
   Parallel

Quiz 20

1. $x = -2$ makes $|x + 2| = 0$.
   $y = 0$ when $x = -2$.
   The vertex is (–2, 0).

2. $x = 1$ makes $|x - 1| = 0$.
   $y = 3$ when $x = 1$.
   The vertex is (1, 3).

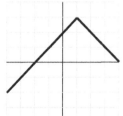

3. Vertex: (0, –5)
   The graph opens up.

4. Vertex: (–3, 0)
   The graph opens down.

5. Vertex: (4, 2)
   The graph opens up.

Quiz 21

1. $m = \dfrac{4-7}{-2-3} = \dfrac{3}{5}$

2. $m = \dfrac{3-5}{-2-4} = \dfrac{1}{3}$
   Given $m = 1/3$
   Perpendicular $m = -3$

3. The line vertical.
   $x = 4$

4.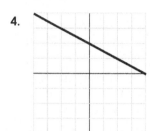

5.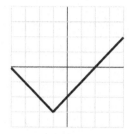

Quiz 22

1. $m = -1$, y-int $= 2$
   $y = -x + 2$

2. $m = 4$, y-int $= 0$
   $y = 4x$

3. $m = 2$, y-int $= -1$
   $y = 2x - 1$

4. $m = 1/3$, y-int $= 1$
   $y = \dfrac{1}{3}x + 1$

5. $m = -3$, y-int $= 3$
   $y = -3x + 3$

Quiz 23

1. $y = -x + b$ $m = -1$
   $-3 = -8 + b$ Use $(8, -3)$ to find b.
   $b = 5$
   $y = -x + 5$ Write $y = mx + b$.

2. $m = \dfrac{9-(-6)}{1-(-2)} = 5$
   $y = 5x + b$
   $9 = 5(1) + b$
   $b = 4$
   $y = 5x + 4$

3. $m = \dfrac{3-3}{10-(-5)} = 0$
   $y = 0x + b$
   $3 = 0(-5) + b$
   $b = 3$
   $y = 3$

4. Given $m = -2$
   Parallel $m = -2$
   $y = -2x + b$
   $-7 = -2(6) + b$
   $b = 5$
   $y = -2x + 5$

5. Given $m = 4/3$
   Perpendicular $m = -3/4$
   $y = -\dfrac{3}{4}x + b$
   $-4 = -\dfrac{3}{4}(8) + b$
   $b = 2$
   $y = -\dfrac{3}{4}x + 2$

Quiz 24

1. $y - 7 = 4(x - 2)$

2. $m = \dfrac{4-(-1)}{-4-(-3)} = -5$
   $y + 1 = -5(x + 3)$

3. $m = \dfrac{0-8}{3-(-5)} = -1$
   $y - 8 = -(x + 5)$

4. Given $m = 1/2$
   Parallel $m = 1/2$
   $y + 4 = \dfrac{1}{2}(x - 6)$

5. Given $m = -1/3$
   Perpendicular $m = 3$
   $y + 8 = 3(x + 5)$

Quiz 25

1. $y - 5 = -3(x + 1)$
   $y = -3x + 2$
   $3x + y = 2$

2. $m = \dfrac{-1-3}{4-(-6)} = -\dfrac{2}{5}$
   $y - 3 = -\dfrac{2}{5}(x + 6)$
   $y = -\dfrac{2}{5}x + \dfrac{3}{5}$
   $2x + 5y = 3$

3. $m = \dfrac{-2-0}{-5-7} = \dfrac{1}{6}$
   $y - 0 = \dfrac{1}{6}(x - 7)$
   $y = \dfrac{1}{6}x - \dfrac{7}{6}$
   $x - 6y = 7$

4. Given $m =$ undefined
   Parallel $m =$ undefined
   The line is vertical and passes through $(3, -4)$.
   $x = 3$

5. Given $m = -3/2$
   Perpendicular $m = 2/3$
   $y - 5 = \dfrac{2}{3}(x - 5)$
   $y = \dfrac{2}{3}x + \dfrac{5}{3}$
   $2x - 3y = -5$

Quiz 26

1. a. $m = 8$ and $b = 10$, so $y = 8x + 10$.
   b. When $x = 4$, $y = 42$. It will cost $42.

2. a. $m = 42$ and $b = 30$, so $y = 42x + 30$.
   b. When $x = 3$, $y = 156$. It will cost $156.

3. a. $m = 7$ and $b = 0$, so $y = 7x$.
   b. When $x = 15$, $y = 105$. There will be 105 gallons.

4. a. $m = 24 + 6 = 30$ and $b = 50$, so $y = 30x + 50$.
   b. When $x = 6$, $y = 230$. It will cost $230.

5. a. $m = -60$ and $b = 1500$, so $y = -60x + 1500$.
   b. When $y = 0$, $x = 25$. It will take 25 minutes.

Quiz 27

1. a. $5x$ = amount from fives
        y = amount from ones
        Total amount = 64, so $5x + y = 64$.
    b. When $y = 9$, $x = 11$. She has 11 fives.

2. a. $6x$ = cost of watermelons
        $2y$ = cost of mangos
        Total cost = 30, so $6x + 2y = 30$.
    b. When $x = 3$, $y = 6$. She can buy 6 mangos.

3. a. $4x$ = points form 4-point questions
        $8y$ = points from 8-point questions
        Total points = 100, so $4x + 8y = 100$.
    b. When $x = 11$, $y = 7$. There are 7 8-point questions.

4. a. $12x$ = cost of adult tickets
        $10y$ = cost of child tickets
        Total cost = 98, so $12x + 10y = 98$.
    b. When $x = 4$, $y = 5$. They bought 5 child tickets.

5. a. $2x$ = number of seats from 2-seat tables
        $6y$ = number of seats from 6-seat tables
        Total number of seats = 78, so $2x + 6y = 78$.
    b. When $x = 15$, $y = 8$. There are 8 6-seat tables.

Quiz 28

1. $m = 1/4$, y-int = 1
    $$y = \frac{1}{4}x + 1$$
    $$x - 4y = -4$$

2. $y + 7 = -3(x - 5)$
    $$y = -3x + 8$$
    $$3x + y = 8$$

3. $$m = \frac{-1 - 3}{4 - (-2)} = -\frac{2}{3}$$
    $$y - 3 = -\frac{2}{3}(x + 2)$$
    $$y = -\frac{2}{3}x + \frac{5}{3}$$
    $$2x + 3y = 5$$

4. Given $m = 1/2$
    Perpendicular $m = -2$
    $$y - 5 = -2(x + 6)$$
    $$y = -2x - 7$$
    $$2x + y = -7$$

5. a. $m = -500$ and $b = 7000$, so $y = -500x + 7000$.
    b. When $y = 2500$, $x = 9$. It will take 9 minutes.

Quiz 29

1. The ordered pair **C** makes all the equations true.

2. Solution: (2, 2)

3. Solution: (1, –1)

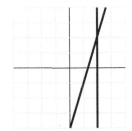

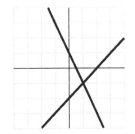

4. Solution: (0, 3)

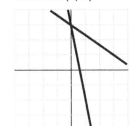

5. Solution: (–2, –2)

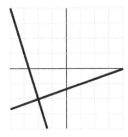

Quiz 30

1. $y = 3x + 2$
    $x + 6(3x + 2) = 12$
    $19x + 12 = 12$
    $x = 0$
    $y = 3(0) + 2 = 2$
    Solution: (0, 2)

2. $y = 4x - 1$
    $5x - 4(4x - 1) = -7$
    $-11x + 4 = -7$
    $x = 1$
    $y = 4(1) - 1 = 3$
    Solution: (1, 3)

3. $x = -3y - 9$
    $3(-3y - 9) - 2y = -5$
    $-11y - 27 = -5$
    $y = -2$
    $x = -3(-2) - 9 = -3$
    Solution: (–3, –2)

4. $x = 2y + 13$
    $(2y + 13) + 5y = -15$
    $7y + 13 = -15$
    $y = -4$
    $x = 2(-4) + 13 = 5$
    Solution: (5, –4)

5. $y = -3x + 2$
    $2x - 3(-3x + 2) = 27$
    $11x - 6 = 27$
    $x = 3$
    $y = -3(3) + 2 = -7$
    Solution: (3, –7)

Quiz 31

1. eq1 – eq2
    $10y = 20$
    $y = 2$
    $x + 8(2) = 13$
    $x = -3$
    Solution: (–3, 2)

2. eq1 × 2 + eq2
    $11x = 22$
    $x = 2$
    $3(2) - y = 15$
    $y = -9$
    Solution: (2, –9)

3. eq1 – eq2 × 3
    $-7x = 42$
    $x = -6$
    $2(-6) + 6y = 0$
    $y = 2$
    Solution: (–6, 2)

4. eq1 × 3 + eq2 × 4
    $25x = 25$
    $x = 1$
    $3(1) + 4y = -9$
    $y = -3$
    Solution: (1, –3)

5. eq1 × 2 + eq2
    $7x = -35$
    $x = -5$
    $2(-5) - 5y = -30$
    $y = 4$
    Solution: (–5, 4)

Quiz 32

1. $y = -x + 8$
   $x - 9(-x + 8) = 8$
   $10x - 72 = 8$
   $x = 8$
   $y = -8 + 8 = 0$
   Solution: (8, 0)

2. eq1 + eq2
   $8x = 32$
   $x = 4$
   $3(4) + 2y = 14$
   $y = 1$
   Solution: (4, 1)

3. eq1 – eq2 × 2
   $-9y = 36$
   $y = -4$
   $4x + 5(-4) = 8$
   $x = 7$
   Solution: (7, –4)

4. $y = 3x - 12$
   $6x + 5(3x - 12) = 3$
   $21x - 60 = 3$
   $x = 3$
   $y = 3(3) - 12 = -3$
   Solution: (3, –3)

5. eq1 × 2 – eq2
   $20y = 20$
   $y = 1$
   $2x + 7(1) = 25$
   $x = 9$
   Solution: (9, 1)

Quiz 33

1. **C** has no solution.

2. **B** ($m = 2$, y-int = –5)

3. $y = 2x - 9$
   $x + 5(2x - 9) = -1$
   $11x - 45 = -1$
   $x = 4$
   $y = 2(4) - 9 = -1$
   Solution: (4, –1)

4. eq1 × 2 + eq2
   $19x = 0$
   $x = 0$
   $5(0) - y = -7$
   $y = 7$
   Solution: (0, 7)

5. eq × 2 + eq2 × 3
   $17x = 85$
   $x = 5$
   $4(5) + 3y = 11$
   $y = -3$
   Solution: (5, –3)

Quiz 34

1. x = tens place digit, y = ones place digit
   $x + y = 10$ and $(10x + y) + 18 = 10y + x$
   Solve the system, and you get $x = 4$ and $y = 6$.
   The number is 46.

2. x = number of quarters, y = number of dimes
   $y = x + 8$ and $0.25x + 0.1y = 3.60$
   Solve the system, and you get $x = 8$ and $y = 16$.
   Leah has 8 quarters and 16 dimes.

3. x = Max's age, y = Kate's age
   $x + y = 32$ and $x - 7 = 2(y - 7)$
   Solve the system, and you get $x = 19$ and $y = 13$.
   Max is 19 years old. Kate is 13 years old.

4. x = # of 4-seat tables, y = # of 6-seat tables
   $x + y = 20$ and $4x + 6y = 92$
   Solve the system, and you get $x = 14$ and $y = 6$.
   14 tables seat 4 people and 6 tables seat 6 people.

5. x = price of a muffin, y = price of a cookie
   $6x + 3y = 10.20$ and $3x + 12y = 11.40$
   Solve the system, and you get $x = 1.4$ and $y = 0.6$.
   Muffins cost $1.40 each and cookies cost $0.60 each.

Quiz 35

1. x = time spent in bus 1
   y = time spent in bus 2
   Total travel time = 5 hours, so $x + y = 5$.
   Distance traveled in bus 1 + distance traveled in bus 2 = 332, so $64x + 70y = 332$.
   Solve the system, and you get $x = 3$ and $y = 2$.
   Lynn spent 3 hours in the first bus and 2 hours in the second bus.

2. x = speed of the plane in still air
   y = speed of the wind
   $x + y$ = speed of the plane flying with the wind
   $x - y$ = speed of the plane flying against the wind
   Distance with the wind = 2700, so $9(x + y) = 2700$.
   Distance against the wind = 2700, $10(x - y) = 2700$.
   Solve the system, and you get $x = 285$ and $y = 15$.
   The speed of the airplane in still air would be 285 mph, and the speed of the wind was 15 mph.

3. x = speed of the boat in still water
   y = speed of the current
   $x + y$ = speed of the boat going downstream
   $x - y$ = speed of the boat going upstream
   Distance = 120, so $3(x + y) = 120$ and $4(x - y) = 120$.
   Solve the system, and you get $x = 35$ and $y = 5$.
   The speed of the boat in still water would be 35 km/h, and the speed of the current was 5 km/h.

4. x = speed of train 1, y = speed of train 2
   One is 20 mph faster than the other, so $y = x + 20$.
   Distance train 1 travels in 3 hours + distance train 2 travels in 3 hours = 810, so $3x + 3y = 810$.
   Solve the system, and you get $x = 125$ and $y = 145$.
   One travels at 125 mph and the other at 145 mph.

5. x = speed of plane 1, y = speed of plane 2
   One is 40 mph faster than the other, so $y = x + 40$.
   Distance plan 1 travels in 2.5 hours + distance plan 2 travels in 2.5 hours = 1600, so $2.5x + 2.5y = 1600$.
   Solve the system, and you get $x = 300$ and $y = 340$.
   One travels at 300 mph and the other at 340 mph.

Quiz 36

1. Let x = liters of water

    $x + 180$ = liters of 18% solution

    Salt in 25% solution = salt in 18% solution,
    so $0.25 \times 180 = 0.18(x + 180)$.

    Solve for x, and you get $x = 70$.

    We need to add 70 liters of water.

2. x = gallons of 20% solution

    y = gallons of 50% solution

    Amount of the mixture = 15, so $x + y = 15$.

    Alcohol in 20% solution + alcohol in 50% solution
    = alcohol in the mixture, so $0.2x + 0.5y = 0.4 \times 15$.

    Solve the system, and you get $x = 5$ and $y = 10$.

    Five gallons of the 20% solution and 10 gallons of the
    50% solution should be mixed.

3. x = ounces of 15% solution

    y = ounces of 30% solution

    Amount of the mixture = 30, so $x + y = 30$.

    Acid in 15% solution + acid in 30% solution
    = acid in the mixture, so $0.15x + 0.3y = 0.24 \times 30$.

    Solve the system, and you get $x = 12$ and $y = 18$.

    12 ounces of the 15% solution and 18 ounces of the
    30% solution should be mixed.

4. x = pounds of coffee A

    y = pounds of coffee B

    Amount of the mixture = 18, so $x + y = 18$.

    Cost of coffee A + cost of coffee B
    = cost of the mixture, so $15x + 12y = 13 \times 18$.

    Solve the system, and you get $x = 6$ and $y = 12$.

    Six pounds of coffee A and 12 pounds of coffee B
    should be mixed.

5. x = pounds of walnuts, y = pounds of almonds

    Amount of the mixture = 25, so $x + y = 25$.

    Cost of walnuts + cost of almonds
    = cost of the mixture, so $4.5x + 6y = 5.1 \times 25$.

    Solve the system, and you get $x = 15$ and $y = 10$.

    15 pounds of walnuts and 10 pounds of almonds
    should be used.

Quiz 37

1. $x = -4$
    $4(-4) + 7y = 5$
    $y = 3$
    Solution: $(-4, 3)$

2. $x = -3y - 1$
    $3(-3y - 1) - 2y = 19$
    $y = -2$
    $x = -3(-2) - 1 = 5$
    Solution: $(5, -2)$

3. x = number of adults, y = number of children

    A total of 9 tickets, so $x + y = 9$.

    Total cost = 98, so $12x + 10y = 98$.

    Solve the system, and you get $x = 4$ and $y = 5$.

    There were 4 adults and 5 children in the group.

4. x = speed of the boat in still water

    y = speed of the current

    $x + y$ = speed of the boat going downstream

    $x - y$ = speed of the boat going upstream

    Distance = 16, so $2(x + y) = 16$ and $4(x - y) = 16$.

    Solve the system, and you get $x = 6$ and $y = 2$.

    The speed of the boat in still water would be 6 mph,
    and the speed of the current was 2 mph.

5. x = ounces of 12% juice, y = ounces of 20% juice

    Amount of the mixture = 16, so $x + y = 16$.

    Pure juice in 12% juice + pure juice in 20% juice
    = pure juice in the mixture, so $0.12x + 0.2y = 0.18 \times 16$.

    Solve the system, and you get $x = 4$ and $y = 12$.

    Four ounces of the 12% juice and 12 ounces of the 20%
    juice should be mixed.

Quiz 38

1.

2. Add 1 to both sides: $7x \le -21$

    Divide both sides by 7: $x \le -3$

3. Simplify each side: $-8x + 10 > 8$

    Subtract 10 from each side: $-8x > -2$

    Divide both sides by –8
    and flip the inequality sign: $x < \dfrac{1}{4}$

4. Multiply both sides by 4: $2x + 3 < 4x - 2$

    Subtract $4x$ from both sides: $-2x + 3 < -2$

    Subtract 3 from both sides: $-2x < -5$

    Divide both sides by –2
    and flip the inequality sign: $x > \dfrac{5}{2}$

5. x = the greater integer $2x \le 36$

    $(x - 1) + x \le 35$ $x \le 18$

    $2x - 1 \le 35$ The answer is 18.

Quiz 39

1.

2. Subtract 3 from all sides: $-10 \le 2x < 8$

    Divide all sides by 2: $-5 \le x < 4$

3. 1st inequality: 2nd inequality:

$x \leq -4$ $3x < 15$

                              $x < 5$

1st inequality AND 2nd inequality: $x \leq -4$

4. 1st inequality: 2nd inequality:

$-4x - 10 > 6$ $2 + 6x < 8$

$-4x > 16$ $6x < 6$

$x < -4$ $x < 1$

1st inequality OR 2nd inequality: $x < 1$

5. Multiply all sides by 10: $3 \leq 5 - 6x < 8$

Subtract 5 from all sides: $-2 \leq -6x < 3$

Divide all sides by –6
and flip the sign: $-\dfrac{1}{2} < x \leq \dfrac{1}{3}$

Quiz 40

1.

2. Rewrite using AND: $-3 \leq x + 5 \leq 3$

Solve for x: $-8 \leq x \leq -2$

3. Rewrite using OR: $2x - 5 < -7$ or $2x - 5 > 7$

Solve for x: $2x < -2$ or $2x > 12$

                       $x < -1$ or $x > 6$

4. Isolate the bars: $|1 - 2x| \geq 1$

Rewrite using OR: $1 - 2x \leq -1$ or $1 - 2x \geq 1$

Solve for x: $-2x \leq -2$ or $-2x \geq 0$

                  $x \geq 1$ or $x \leq 0$

                  $x \leq 0$ or $x \geq 1$

5. Isolate the bars: $2|4 - x| < 12$

                   $|4 - x| < 6$

Rewrite using AND: $-6 < 4 - x < 6$

Solve for x: $-10 < -x < 2$

                  $-2 < x < 10$

Quiz 41

1. The ordered pair **D** does not satisfy the inequality.

2. 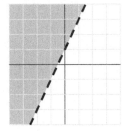   **3.**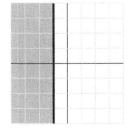

4. 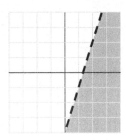   **5.**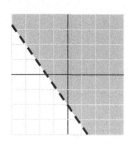

Quiz 42

1. The system **B** has no overlapping region when graphed, so it has no solution.

2. The solution set to $y \geq -x$ is P and S.

The solution set to $y < 2x - 3$ is S and R.

The solution set to the system is region **S**.

3. The solution set to $x + 2y < 4$ is Q and R.

The solution set to $x + 2y > -4$ is P and Q.

The solution set to the system is region **Q**.

4. 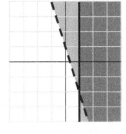   **5.**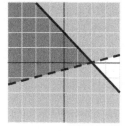

Quiz 43

1. $2x + 6 > x + 4$ **2.** $-2 \leq 1 - 3x < 10$

    $x + 6 > 4$ $-3 \leq -3x < 9$

    $x > -2$ $-3 < x \leq 1$

3. $|5 - 2x| > 5$ $\Rightarrow$ $x > 5$ or $x < 0$

    $5 - 2x < -5$ or $5 - 2x > 5$ $x < 0$ or $x > 5$

    $-2x < -10$ or $-2x > 0$

4. The line is $y = -2x$, so the answer is C or D.

(1, 0) is a solution, so the answer is **D**.

5. The solid line $y = -1$, so the answer is C or D.

(0, 0) is a solution, so the answer is **C**.

Quiz 48

1. Function because each input has exactly one output.

2. Function because each input has exactly one output.

3. Not a function because input 1 has two outputs.

4. Not a function because input 3 has two outputs.

5. Function because it passes the vertical line test.

Quiz 49

1. The sum, S, is the dependent variable.
   The number of sides, n, is the independent variable.

2. Domain: {1, 2, 3}
   Range: {−2, −1, 0, 1, 2}
   Not a function

3. Domain: {0, 1, 2, 3, 4}
   Range: {3}
   Function

4. Domain: $-5 < x < -1$
   Range: $-1 < y < 2$
   Function

5. Domain: $-3 \leq x \leq 1$
   Range: $-2 \leq y < 2$
   Not a function

Quiz 50

1. $f(-4) = (-4)^2 - 7$
   $f(-4) = 9$
   $n = 9$

2. $g(n) = 3n + 5 = -10$
   $3n = -15$
   $n = -5$

3. $h(n) = |n| - 4 = 8$
   $|n| = 12$
   $n = 12$ or $n = -12$

4. $p(4) = 0, p(1) = 1$
   $p(4) - p(1) = -1$
   $n = -1$

5. $p(2) = 0, P(4) = 0$
   $n = 2, n = 4$

Quiz 51

1. **B** is linear because it can be written in slope-intercept form. Note that $x = 5$ is a vertical line which is not a function.

2. Nonlinear
   The graph is not a straight line.

3. Linear
   $y = \frac{1}{2}x + 1$

4. Linear
   $y = x + 4$

5. Nonlinear
   The rate of change is not constant.

Quiz 52

1. **A** is exponential. C is quadratic. D is linear.

2. Exponential

3. Quadratic

4. Linear because the first differences are constant.

5. Exponential because the ratios are constant.

Quiz 53

1. $\dfrac{f(2) - f(-1)}{2 - (-1)} = \dfrac{7 - 1}{2 - (-1)} = 2$

2. $\dfrac{f(4) - f(0)}{4 - 0} = \dfrac{0 - 0}{4 - 0} = 0$

3. $\dfrac{f(6) - f(-3)}{6 - (-3)} = \dfrac{31 - (-5)}{6 - (-3)} = 4$

4. $\dfrac{f(6) - f(2)}{6 - 2} = \dfrac{64 - 4}{6 - 2} = 15$

5. $\dfrac{h(5) - h(0)}{5 - 0} = \dfrac{400 - 0}{5 - 0} = 80 \, feet \, per \, second$

Quiz 54

1. $f(n) = 1$
   $n = 1$

2. $f(n) = -1$
   $n = 3$

3. Set y equal to $f(x)$: $y = x - 1$
   Switch x and y: $x = y - 1$
   Solve for y: $y = x + 1$
   Write in function notation: $f^{-1}(x) = x + 1$

4. $y = -x + 7$
   $x = -y + 7$
   $y = -x + 7$
   $f^{-1}(x) = -x + 7$

5. $y = \frac{1}{2}x + \frac{3}{2}$
   $x = \frac{1}{2}y + \frac{3}{2}$
   $2x = y + 3$
   $y = 2x - 3$
   $f^{-1}(x) = 2x - 3$

Quiz 55

1. Not a function because it fails the vertical line test.

2. Nonlinear because the rate of change is not constant.

3. Quadratic because the second differences are constant.

4. $\dfrac{f(2) - f(-1)}{2 - (-1)} = \dfrac{8 - (-1)}{2 - (-1)} = 3$

5. Set y equal to $f(x)$: $y = 3x - 6$
   Switch x and y: $x = 3y - 6$
   Solve for y: $3y = x + 6$
      $y = \frac{1}{3}x + 2$

   Write in function notation: $f^{-1}(x) = \frac{1}{3}x + 2$

Quiz 56

1. **A** represents direct variation.

2. Plug (2, 8) into $y = kx$: $8 = k(2)$
   Solve for k: $k = 4$
   Find the equation: $y = 4x$

3. Find the equation: Find y when $x = -5$:
   $-9 = k(3); k = -3$ $y = -3(-5)$
   $y = -3x$ $y = 15$

4. Find the equation: Find x when $y = 2$:
   $1 = k(5); \ k = 1/5$ $2 = (1/5)x$
   $y = (1/5)x$ $x = 10$

5. x = time in minutes, y = number of words

$80 = 2k$, so $k = 40$ and $y = 40x$.

When $x = 5$, $y = 40(5) = 200$.

Emma will type 200 words in 5 minutes.

Quiz 57

1. **B** represents inverse variation.

2. Plug (2, 3) into $xy = k$: $\quad 2 \times 3 = k$

Write the equation: $\quad xy = 6$ or $y = 6/x$

3. Find the equation: $\quad\vdash\!\!>$ Find y when $x = 5$:

$(-2) \times 10 = k \qquad\qquad 5y = -20$

$xy = -20$ or $y = -20/x\dashv \qquad y = -4$

4. Find the equation: $\quad\vdash\!\!>$ Find x when $y = 3$:

$2 \times 6 = k \qquad\qquad\qquad x(3) = 12$

$xy = 12$ or $y = 12/x \quad\dashv\qquad x = 4$

5. x = speed, y = time

$k = 60$ mph $\times$ 1/3 hour = 20, so $xy = 20$ or $y = 20/x$.

When $x = 50$, $y = 2/5 = 0.4$.

It will take 0.4 hour, or 24 minutes.

Quiz 58

1. 13 and 15 $\qquad\qquad$ **2.** 5, 2, –1, –4, –7

3. $a_n = a_1 + (n-1)d$ $\quad$ **4.** $a_1 = 8, d = -5$

$\quad a_n = 10 + 6(n-1) \qquad\qquad a_n = 8 - 5(n-1)$

$\quad\quad = 6n + 4 \qquad\qquad\qquad\quad = -5n + 13$

5. $a_1 = 16, d = 7$

$\quad a_n = 16 + 7(n-1)$

$\quad\quad = 7n + 9$

Quiz 59

1. 32 and 64 $\qquad\qquad$ **2.** 2, 6, 18, 54, 162

3. $a_n = a_1 r^{n-1}$ $\qquad\quad$ **4.** $a_1 = 2, r = 5$

$\quad a_n = 3(2)^{n-1} \qquad\qquad\quad a_n = 2(5)^{n-1}$

5. $a_1 = 1, r = -3$

$\quad a_n = (-3)^{n-1}$

Quiz 60

1. Arithmetic sequence $\quad$ **2.** Geometric sequence

$\quad a_1 = 2, d = 7 \qquad\qquad\quad a_1 = 2, r = 3$

$\quad a_n = 2 + 7(n-1) \qquad\quad a_n = 2(3)^{n-1}$

$\quad\quad = 7n - 5$

3. Arithmetic sequence $\quad$ **3.** Geometric sequence

$\quad a_1 = 5, d = -4 \qquad\qquad a_1 = 5, r = 2$

$\quad a_1 = 5, a_n = a_{n-1} - 4 \quad a_1 = 5, a_n = 2a_{n-1}$

5. Geometric sequence

$a_1 = 4, r = -3$

$a_1 = 4, a_n = -3a_{n-1}$

Quiz 61

1. Find the rule: $\quad\vdash\!\!>$ Find the 8th term:

$a_1 = 6, d = 3 \qquad\qquad a_8 = 3(8) + 3 = 27$

$a_n = 6 + 3(n-1)$

$\quad = 3n + 3 \qquad\dashv$

2. Find the rule: $\quad\vdash\!\!>$ Find the 8th term:

$a_1 = 1, r = 2 \qquad\qquad a_8 = (2)^{8-1} = 128$

$a_n = (2)^{n-1} \quad\dashv$

3. 4, 4.7, 5.4, 6.1, 6.8, … is an arithmetic sequence.

$a_1 = 4, d = 0.7$

$a_n = 0.7n + 3.3$

$a_6 = 0.7(6) + 3.3 = 7.5$

The height of the tree will be about 8 feet.

4. The value after the 1st year is 22000 × 0.8 = 17600.

The value after the 2nd year is 17600× 0.8 = 14080.

17600, 14080, 11264, … is a geometric sequence.

$a_1 = 17600, r = 0.8$

$a_n = 17600(0.8)^{n-1}$

$a_5 = 17600(0.8)^{5-1} = 7208.96$

The value of the car will be about $7,209.

5. 68000, 69200, 70400, … is an arithmetic sequence.

$a_1 = 68000, d = 1200$

$a_n = 1200n + 66800$

$a_9 = 1200(9) + 66800 = 77600$

His salary will be $77,600.

Quiz 62

1. Find the equation: $\quad\vdash\!\!>$ Find y when $x = 2$:

$12 = k(4); k = 3 \qquad\qquad y = 3(2) = 6$

$y = 3x$

2. Find the equation: $\quad\vdash\!\!>$ Find x when $y = 2$:

$k = (-5) \times (-4) = 20 \qquad x(2) = 20$

$xy = 20$ or $y = 20/x \quad\dashv\qquad x = 10$

3. Arithmetic sequence $\quad$ **4.** Geometric sequence

$\quad a_1 = 15, d = 2 \qquad\qquad\quad a_1 = 1, r = 5$

$\quad a_n = 15 + 2(n-1) \qquad\quad a_1 = 1, a_n = 5a_{n-1}$

$\quad\quad = 2n + 13$

5. 20, 40, 80, 160, 320, … $\quad\vdash\!\!>\ a_6 = 20(2)^{6-1} = 640$

$a_1 = 20, r = 2 \qquad\qquad\qquad$ There will be 640

$a_n = 20(2)^{n-1} \qquad\dashv$ bacteria.

Quiz 63

1. $\sqrt{6^2} = 6$ 2. $\sqrt[3]{(-4)^3} = -4$

3. $\sqrt[4]{3^4} = 3$

4. $\sqrt{12^2} + \sqrt{4^2} \times \sqrt[3]{(-2)^3} = 12 + 4 \times (-2) = 4$

5. $\left(\sqrt{5^2} + \sqrt[3]{3^3} + \sqrt[5]{2^5}\right) \times \sqrt{0.2^2}$
   $= (5 + 3 + 2) \times 0.2 = 2$

Quiz 64

1. $\sqrt{25 \cdot 2} = 5\sqrt{2}$ 2. $\sqrt{9 \cdot 3} = 3\sqrt{3}$

3. $3\sqrt{4 \cdot 5} = 6\sqrt{5}$ 4. $2\sqrt{16 \cdot 7} = 8\sqrt{7}$

5. $\dfrac{\sqrt{24}}{\sqrt{121}} = \dfrac{\sqrt{4 \cdot 6}}{11} = \dfrac{2\sqrt{6}}{11}$

Quiz 65

1. $\sqrt{x^2} \cdot \sqrt{y^2} = xy$

2. $\sqrt{9 \cdot 5 \cdot x^2 \cdot x} = \sqrt{9} \cdot \sqrt{x^2} \cdot \sqrt{5x} = 3x\sqrt{5x}$

3. $2 \cdot \sqrt{9 \cdot 7 \cdot x^2 \cdot x^2 \cdot y} = 2 \cdot \sqrt{9} \cdot \sqrt{x^2} \cdot \sqrt{x^2} \cdot \sqrt{7y}$
   $= 2 \cdot 3 \cdot x \cdot x \cdot \sqrt{7y} = 6x^2\sqrt{7y}$

4. $-3 \cdot \sqrt{9 \cdot 2 \cdot x^2 \cdot y^2 \cdot y^2 \cdot y}$
   $= -3 \cdot \sqrt{9} \cdot \sqrt{x^2} \cdot \sqrt{y^2} \cdot \sqrt{y^2} \cdot \sqrt{2y}$
   $= -3 \cdot 3 \cdot x \cdot y \cdot y \cdot \sqrt{2y} = -9xy^2\sqrt{2y}$

5. $\dfrac{\sqrt{9}}{\sqrt{x^6y^2z^4}} = \dfrac{3}{\sqrt{x^2 \cdot x^2 \cdot x^2 \cdot y^2 \cdot z^2 \cdot z^2}}$
   $= \dfrac{3}{x \cdot x \cdot x \cdot y \cdot z \cdot z} = \dfrac{3}{x^3yz^2}$

Quiz 66

1. $\left(4\sqrt{3} + \sqrt{3}\right) + \left(2\sqrt{5} - \sqrt{5}\right) = 5\sqrt{3} + \sqrt{5}$

2. $3\sqrt{6} - \sqrt{4 \cdot 6} = 3\sqrt{6} - 2\sqrt{6} = \sqrt{6}$

3. $\sqrt{16 \cdot 2} + \sqrt{9 \cdot 2} = 4\sqrt{2} + 3\sqrt{2} = 7\sqrt{2}$

4. $\sqrt{5^2} - \sqrt{49 \cdot 2} + 3\sqrt{16 \cdot 2}$
   $= 5 - 7\sqrt{2} + 12\sqrt{2} = 5 + 5\sqrt{2}$

5. $\sqrt{25 \cdot 3} + 2\sqrt{9 \cdot 5} - 4\sqrt{9 \cdot 3} - \sqrt{16 \cdot 5}$
   $= 5\sqrt{3} + 6\sqrt{5} - 12\sqrt{3} - 4\sqrt{5} = -7\sqrt{3} + 2\sqrt{5}$

Quiz 67

1. $\sqrt{12} = \sqrt{4 \cdot 3} = 2\sqrt{3}$

2. $\sqrt{40x^2} = \sqrt{4 \cdot 10 \cdot x^2} = 2x\sqrt{10}$

3. $\sqrt{36x^4y^2} = \sqrt{6^2 \cdot x^2 \cdot x^2 \cdot y^2} = 6x^2y$

4. $\dfrac{3}{\sqrt{7}} \cdot \dfrac{\sqrt{7}}{\sqrt{7}} = \dfrac{3\sqrt{7}}{7}$

5. $\sqrt{\dfrac{54x^3}{2x}} = \sqrt{27x^2} = \sqrt{9 \cdot 3 \cdot x^2} = 3x\sqrt{3}$

Quiz 68

1. Isolate the square root: $\sqrt{x} = 4$
   Square both sides: $\left(\sqrt{x}\right)^2 = 4^2$
   Solve and check: $x = 16$

2. Square both sides: $\left(\sqrt{2x-3}\right)^2 = 1^2$
   Solve and check: $2x - 3 = 1$
     $x = 2$

3. Square both sides: $\left(2\sqrt{x+1}\right)^2 = \left(\sqrt{3x+4}\right)^2$
   Solve and check: $4(x+1) = 3x + 4$
     $x = 0$

4. Square both sides: $\left(\sqrt{5x-1}\right)^2 = \left(\sqrt{x-9}\right)^2$
   Solve and check: $5x - 1 = x - 9$
     $x = -2$
   -2 makes the radicands negative, so no solution.

5. Isolate the cube root: $\sqrt[3]{x+9} = -2$
   Cube both sides: $\left(\sqrt[3]{x+9}\right)^3 = (-2)^3$
   Solve and check: $x + 9 = -8$
     $x = -17$

Quiz 69

1. x = side length
   Area = 60, so $x^2 = 60$ and $x = 2\sqrt{15}$.
   The length of one side is $2\sqrt{15}$ inches.

2. Hypotenuse = x, Legs = 3 and 4
   The Pythagorean Theorem gives $3^2 + 4^2 = x^2$.
   $x^2 = 3^2 + 4^2 = 25$; $x = 5$
   The length of the hypotenuse is 5 cm.

3. Hypotenuse = $7\sqrt{2}$, Legs = x and x

   The Pythagorean Theorem gives $x^2 + x^2 = (7\sqrt{2})^2$.

   $2x^2 = 98$; $x^2 = 49$; $x = 7$

   The length of each leg is 7 cm.

4. Diagonal = 8, length = 6, width = x

   The Pythagorean Theorem gives $6^2 + x^2 = 8^2$.

   $x^2 = 64 - 36 = 28$; $x = 2\sqrt{7}$

   The width of the rectangle is $2\sqrt{7}$ inches.

5. $d = \sqrt{(-3-2)^2 + (4-(-6))^2} = \sqrt{125} = 5\sqrt{5}$

Quiz 70

1. $\sqrt{3^2} - \sqrt[4]{2^4} \times \sqrt[5]{(-2)^5} - \sqrt[3]{(-1)^3}$

   $= 3 - 2 \times (-2) - (-1) = 8$

2. $\sqrt{9 \cdot 3 \cdot x^2 \cdot x^2 \cdot x \cdot y^2} = 3x^2 y\sqrt{3x}$

3. $\dfrac{4}{\sqrt{2}} \cdot \dfrac{\sqrt{2}}{\sqrt{2}} + \sqrt{50} = \dfrac{4\sqrt{2}}{2} + \sqrt{25 \cdot 2} = 2\sqrt{2} + 5\sqrt{2} = 7\sqrt{2}$

4. Square both sides: $\left(\sqrt{x+3}\right)^2 = \left(\sqrt{2x-7}\right)^2$

   Solve and check: $x + 3 = 2x - 7$

   $x = 10$

5. x = side length y = diagonal

   Area = 36, so $x^2 = 36$. $6^2 + 6^2 = y^2$

   Solve for x, and $x = 6$. $y = 6\sqrt{2}$

   The side length is 6 cm.   The diagonal is $6\sqrt{2}$ cm.

Quiz 71

1. $\dfrac{1}{3^2} = \dfrac{1}{9}$ 2. 1

3. $\dfrac{5^5}{5^3} = 25$ 4. $\dfrac{6^3}{2 \cdot 6^2} = 3$

5. $\dfrac{10^5}{2^3 \cdot (-5)^4} = 20$

Quiz 72

1. $4x^{3+2} = 4x^5$ 2. $3 \cdot 2 \cdot x^{5-4} = 6x$

3. $20x^{2-5+1} = 20x^{-2} = \dfrac{20}{x^2}$ 4. $x^{5-1-2} = x^2$

5. $\dfrac{8}{-2}x^{3-4-2} = -4x^{-3} = -\dfrac{4}{x^3}$

Quiz 73

1. $2^5 x^{2\times 5} = 32x^{10}$

2. $(-3)^2 x^{-3\times 2} = 9x^{-6} = \dfrac{9}{x^6}$

3. $4^{-3}x^{-4\times -3} = \dfrac{x^{12}}{4^3} = \dfrac{x^{12}}{64}$ 4. $\dfrac{(-2)^3}{x^3} = -\dfrac{8}{x^3}$

5. $\dfrac{3^{-2}}{x^{2\times -2}} = \dfrac{3^{-2}}{x^{-4}} = \dfrac{x^4}{3^2} = \dfrac{x^4}{9}$ or   5. $\left(\dfrac{x^2}{3}\right)^2 = \dfrac{x^4}{3^2} = \dfrac{x^4}{9}$

Quiz 74

1. $1 \cdot 2^3 x^6 = 8x^6$

2. $9x \cdot (-3)^{-2} x^{-10} = 9 \cdot \dfrac{1}{9} \cdot x^{-9} = x^{-9} = \dfrac{1}{x^9}$

   or $\dfrac{9x}{(-3x^5)^2} = \dfrac{9x}{(-3)^2 x^{10}} = \dfrac{9x}{9x^{10}} = \dfrac{1}{x^9}$

3. $(-6)^2 x^6 \cdot 2^{-2} x^6 = \dfrac{(-6)^2}{2^2} \cdot x^{12} = \dfrac{36}{4} \cdot x^{12} = 9x^{12}$

   or $\dfrac{(-6x^3)^2}{(2x^{-3})^2} = \dfrac{(-6)^2 x^6}{2^2 x^{-6}} = \dfrac{36}{4} \cdot x^{12} = 9x^{12}$

4. $\left(\dfrac{3x^2}{x^4}\right)^3 = \left(\dfrac{3}{x^2}\right)^3 = \dfrac{3^3}{x^6} = \dfrac{27}{x^6}$

5. $\dfrac{(-4x^7)^3}{(8x^7)^2} = \dfrac{(-4)^3 x^{21}}{8^2 x^{14}} = \dfrac{-64}{64} \cdot x^7 = -x^7$

Quiz 75

1. 2.4×10^8 2. 5×10^{-7}

3. 0.00049

4. 35×10^{12} 5. 0.25×10^{-3}

   $= 3.5 \times 10^{13}$ $= 2.5 \times 10^{-4}$

Quiz 76

1. $x^{2/3}$ 2. $\sqrt[4]{x^5}$

3. $(3^2)^{1/2} = 3^1 = 3$ 4. $(2^4)^{5/4} = 2^5 = 32$

5. $(10^3)^{-2/3} = 10^{-2} - \dfrac{1}{10^2} = \dfrac{1}{100}$

Quiz 77

1. $x^{1/2 + 2/3} = x^{7/6}$

2. $\left(2^3 x^{1/4}\right)^{4/3} = 2^4 x^{1/3} = 16x^{1/3}$

3. $\left(3^3 x^{3/4}\right)^{2/3} = 3^2 x^{1/2} = 9x^{1/2}$

4. $x^{1/2} \cdot x^{1/3} = x^{5/6} = \sqrt[6]{x^5}$

5. $\dfrac{x^{5/6}}{x^{1/3}} = x^{1/2} = \sqrt{x}$

Quiz 78

1. **B** represents exponential growth.
   C and D represent exponential decay.

2. **C** represents exponential decay.
   B and D represent exponential growth.

3. The equation represents exponential decay because the growth factor is 1/5 which is less than 1.
   B represents exponential decay.

4. $a = 6$ and $b = 1.03$, so $y = 6(1.03)^x$.
   When $x = 5$, $y = 6(1.03)^5 = 6.95564...$
   It will cost about $6.96.

5. $a = 18000$ and $b = 0.85$, so $y = 18000(0.85)^x$.
   When $x = 10$, $y = 18000(0.85)^{10} = 3543.73927...$
   It will be worth about $3,543.74.

Quiz 79

1. $\dfrac{6^3}{3^2} = 24$

2. $(4^3)^{2/3} = 4^2 = 16$

3. $4x^5 \cdot 3x^0 \cdot 6^{-1}x^{-2} = \dfrac{4 \cdot 3}{6} \cdot x^{5+0-2} = 2x^3$

4. $\left(10^3 x^{3/4}\right)^{1/3} = 10x^{1/4}$

5. $30 \times 10^7 = 3 \times 10^8$

Quiz 80

1. **B** not a polynomial because of the exponent –2.

2. The degree is 4 and the leading coefficient is 3.

3. $(2x - 4x) + (7 - (-2)) = -2x + 9$

4. $x^2 + (-3x + 7x) + (5 - 5) = x^2 + 4x$

5. $x^3 + (-2x^2 - x^2) + \left(4x - (-3x)\right) + (9 - 2)$
   $= x^3 - 3x^2 + 7x + 7$

Quiz 81

1. $(-2)(-5)x^{4+2} = 10x^6$

2. $3x^2(x^2) + 3x^2(-2x) + 3x^2(3)$
   $= 3x^4 - 6x^3 + 9x^2$

3. $x^2 + 3x + 4x + 12$
   $= x^2 + 7x + 12$

4. $5x^2 + x - 10x - 2$
   $= 5x^2 - 9x - 2$

5. $4x^2 - 2x + 2x - 1$
   $= 4x^2 - 1$

Quiz 82

1. $2x^2 + 6x - x - 3$
   $= 2x^2 + 5x - 3$

2. $x^3 + 2x^2 - 5x + 4x^2 + 8x - 20$
   $= x^3 + 6x^2 + 3x - 20$

3. $3x^3 + 6x^2 - x^2 - 2x + 4x + 8$
   $= 3x^3 + 5x^2 + 2x + 8$

4. $x^4 - x^3 + x^2 + 2x^3 - 2x^2 + 2x - 3x^2 + 3x - 3$
   $= x^4 + x^3 - 4x^2 + 5x - 3$

5. $(x^2 - x + 2x - 2)(4x + 1)$
   $= (x^2 + x - 2)(4x + 1)$
   $= 4x^3 + x^2 + 4x^2 + x - 8x - 2$
   $= 4x^3 + 5x^2 - 7x - 2$

Quiz 83

1. $x^2 + 2 \cdot x \cdot 3 + 3^2$
   $= x^2 + 6x + 9$

2. $(3x)^2 - 2 \cdot 3x \cdot 2 + 2^2$
   $= 9x^2 - 12x + 4$

3. $(2x)^2 - 5^2$
   $= 4x^2 - 25$

4. $(40 + 3)^2$
   $= 40^2 + 2 \cdot 40 \cdot 3 + 3^2$
   $= 1600 + 240 + 9$
   $= 1849$

5. $(30 - 2)(30 + 2)$
   $= 30^2 - 2^2$
   $= 900 - 4$
   $= 896$

Quiz 84

1. $x^2 - 3x + 2x - 6$
   $= x^2 - x - 6$

2. $x^2 - 2 \cdot x \cdot 3 + 3^2$
   $= x^2 - 6x + 9$

3. $(3x)^2 - 4^2$
   $= 9x^2 - 16$

4. $(2x)^2 + 2 \cdot 2x \cdot 5 + 5^2$
   $= 4x^2 + 20x + 25$

5. $4x^2 + 3x - 16x - 12$
   $= 4x^2 - 13x - 12$

Quiz 85

1. $\dfrac{25}{-5} \cdot x^{4-3} = -5x$

2. $\dfrac{6x^3}{3x} - \dfrac{12x^2}{3x} + \dfrac{9x}{3x} = 2x^2 - 4x + 3$

3.
$$
\begin{array}{r}
x - 2 \\
x - 3 \overline{)\, x^2 - 5x + 6} \\
\underline{x^2 - 3x} \\
-2x + 6 \\
\underline{-2x + 6} \\
0
\end{array}
$$
Answer: $x - 2$

4.
$$
\begin{array}{r}
x - 4 \\
3x + 1 \overline{)\, 3x^2 - 11x - 4} \\
\underline{3x^2 + \ \ x} \\
-12x - 4 \\
\underline{-12x - 4} \\
0
\end{array}
$$
Answer: $x - 4$

5.

$$2x - 1 \enclose{longdiv}{8x^2 + 6x - 5}$$
quotient: $4x + 5$
$$8x^2 - 4x$$
$$\overline{10x - 5}$$
$$10x - 5$$
$$\overline{0} \qquad \text{Answer: } 4x + 5$$

Quiz 86

1.

$$x + 2 \enclose{longdiv}{x^2 + 4x + 5}$$
quotient: $x + 2$
$$x^2 + 2x$$
$$\overline{2x + 5}$$
$$2x + 4$$
$$\overline{1}$$
Answer:
$$x + 2 + \frac{1}{x + 2}$$

2.

$$x - 3 \enclose{longdiv}{x^2 - 5x + 4}$$
quotient: $x - 2$
$$x^2 - 3x$$
$$\overline{-2x + 4}$$
$$-2x + 6$$
$$\overline{-2}$$
Answer:
$$x - 2 - \frac{2}{x - 3}$$

3.

$$3x - 1 \enclose{longdiv}{9x^2 - 6x + 4}$$
quotient: $3x - 1$
$$9x^2 - 3x$$
$$\overline{-3x + 4}$$
$$-3x + 1$$
$$\overline{3}$$
Answer:
$$3x - 1 + \frac{3}{3x - 1}$$

4.

$$2x + 3 \enclose{longdiv}{4x^2 + 0x + 1}$$
quotient: $2x - 3$
$$4x^2 + 6x$$
$$\overline{-6x + 1}$$
$$-6x - 9$$
$$\overline{10}$$
Answer:
$$2x - 3 + \frac{10}{2x + 3}$$

5.

$$3x + 1 \enclose{longdiv}{9x^2 + 0x - 5}$$
quotient: $3x - 1$
$$9x^2 + 3x$$
$$\overline{-3x - 5}$$
$$-3x - 1$$
$$\overline{-4}$$
Answer:
$$3x - 1 - \frac{4}{3x + 1}$$

Quiz 87

1. $(5x^2 - 3x^2) + (-2x - x) + (3 - (-1))$
$= 2x^2 - 3x + 4$

2. $2x^2 - x + 6x - 3$
$= 2x^2 + 5x - 3$

3. $x^2 - 2 \cdot x \cdot 2 + 2^2$
$= x^2 - 4x + 4$

4.

$$x - 5 \enclose{longdiv}{2x^2 - 9x - 5}$$
quotient: $2x + 1$
$$2x^2 - 10x$$
$$\overline{x - 5}$$
$$x - 5$$
$$\overline{0}$$
Answer:
$$2x + 1$$

5.

$$x - 6 \enclose{longdiv}{x^2 - 8x + 9}$$
quotient: $x - 2$
$$x^2 - 6x$$
$$\overline{-2x + 9}$$
$$-2x + 12$$
$$\overline{-3}$$
Answer:
$$x - 2 - \frac{3}{x - 6}$$

Quiz 93

1. $3(x - 3)$

2. $4x(3x + 4)$

3. $x^2 y(7y - 2)$

4. $3x^2(5x^3 + 4x - 3)$

5. $xy(x^2 y^2 + 6xy - 10)$

Quiz 94

1. $x^2(x - 3) + 2(x - 3)$
$= (x - 3)(x^2 + 2)$

2. $2x^2(x + 4) + 3(x + 4)$
$= (x + 4)(2x^2 + 3)$

3. $2x^3(3x^2 - 5) - (3x^2 - 5)$
$= (3x^2 - 5)(2x^3 - 1)$

4. $2(x^3 + x^2 + 3x + 3)$
$= 2[x^2(x + 1) + 3(x + 1)]$
$= 2(x + 1)(x^2 + 3)$

5. $x^2(5x^3 - x^2 - 10x + 2)$
$= x^2[x^2(5x - 1) - 2(5x - 1)]$
$= x^2(5x - 1)(x^2 - 2)$

Quiz 95

1. $c = 2 \times 3 = 6$
$b = 2 + 3 = 5$
$(x + 2)(x + 3)$

2. $c = -1 \times -3 = 3$
$b = -1 + -3 = -4$
$(x - 1)(x - 3)$

3. $c = -2 \times 4 = -8$
$b = -2 + 4 = 2$
$(x - 2)(x + 4)$

4. $c = 2 \times 5 = 10$
$b = 2 + 5 = 7$
$(x + 2)(x + 5)$

5. $c = -4 \times 7 = -28$
$b = -4 + 7 = 3$
$(x - 4)(x + 7)$

Quiz 96

1. $(x + 4)(x + 6)$

2. $(x + 2)(x - 8)$

3. $2(x^2 - 2x - 15)$
$= 2(x + 3)(x - 5)$

4. $4(x^2 + 5x - 6)$
$= 4(x - 1)(x + 6)$

5. $3(x^2 - 9x + 14)$
$= 3(x - 2)(x - 7)$

Quiz 97

1. Set up $(x \quad)(2x \quad)$, then check factors of 1.

Possible factorization: Middle term:

$(x + 1)(2x + 1)$ $x + 2x = 3x$ ✓

$(x - 1)(2x - 1)$ $-x - 2x = -3x$

The answer is $(x + 1)(2x + 1)$.

2. Set up $(x \quad)(8x \quad)$ and $(2x \quad)(4x \quad)$, then check factors of 3.

Possible factorization: Middle term:

Possible factorization:	Middle term:
$(x + 1)(8x + 3)$	$3x + 8x = 11x$
$(2x + 1)(4x + 3)$	$6x + 4x = 10x$
$(x - 1)(8x - 3)$	$-3x - 8x = -11x$
$(2x - 1)(4x - 3)$	$-6x - 4x = -10x$
$(x + 3)(8x + 1)$	$x + 24x = 25x$
$(2x + 3)(4x + 1)$	$2x + 12x = 14x$
$(x - 3)(8x - 1)$	$-x - 24x = -25x$
$(2x - 3)(4x - 1)$	$-2x - 12x = -14x$ ✓

The answer is $(2x - 3)(4x - 1)$.

3. Set up $(x \quad)(3x \quad)$, then check factors of −8.

Possible factorization:	Middle term:
$(x + 1)(3x - 8)$	$-8x + 3x = -5x$
$(x - 1)(3x + 8)$	$8x - 3x = 5x$
$(x + 2)(3x - 4)$	$-4x + 6x = 2x$
$(x - 2)(3x + 4)$	$4x - 6x = -2x$
$(x + 4)(3x - 2)$	$-2x + 12x = 10x$
$(x - 4)(3x + 2)$	$2x - 12x = -10x$ ✓
$(x + 8)(3x - 1)$	$-x + 24x = 23x$
$(x - 8)(3x + 1)$	$x - 24x = -23x$

The answer is $(x - 4)(3x + 2)$.

4. Set up $(x \quad)(5x \quad)$, then check factors of −9.

Possible factorization:	Middle term:
$(x + 1)(5x - 9)$	$-9x + 5x = -4x$
$(x - 1)(5x + 9)$	$9x - 5x = 4x$
$(x + 3)(5x - 3)$	$-3x + 15x = 12x$ ✓
$(x - 3)(5x + 3)$	$3x - 15x = -12x$
$(x + 9)(5x - 1)$	$-x + 45x = 44x$
$(x - 9)(5x + 1)$	$x - 45x = -44x$

The answer is $(x + 3)(5x - 3)$.

5. Set up $(x \quad)(9x \quad)$ and $(3x \quad)(3x \quad)$, then check factors of 16.

Possible factorization:	Middle term:
$(x + 1)(9x + 16)$	$16x + 9x = 25x$
$(3x + 1)(3x + 16)$	$48x + 3x = 51x$
$(x - 1)(9x - 16)$	$-16x - 9x = -25x$
$(3x - 1)(3x - 16)$	$-48x - 3x = -51x$
...	...
$(x + 4)(9x + 4)$	$4x + 36x = 40x$
$(3x + 4)(3x + 4)$	$12x + 12x = 24x$
$(x - 4)(9x - 4)$	$-4x - 36x = -40x$
$(3x - 4)(3x - 4)$	$-12x - 12x = -24x$ ✓
...	...

The answer is $(3x - 4)^2$.

Quiz 98

1. $ac = -36, b = -5$ $6x^2 + 4x - 9x - 6$
$rs = 4 \times -9 = -36$ $= 2x(3x + 2) - 3(3x + 2)$
$r + s = 4 + -9 = -5$ $= (3x + 2)(2x - 3)$

2. $ac = -12, b = -11$ $3x^2 + x - 12x - 4$
$rs = 1 \times -12 = -12$ $= x(3x + 1) - 4(3x + 1)$
$r + s = 1 + -12 = -11$ $= (3x + 1)(x - 4)$

3. $ac = 28, b = 16$ $4x^2 + 2x + 14x + 7$
$rs = 2 \times 14 = 28$ $= 2x(2x + 1) + 7(2x + 1)$
$r + s = 2 + 14 = 16$ $= (2x + 1)(2x + 7)$

4. $ac = 60, b = 19$ $5x^2 + 4x + 15x + 12$
$rs = 4 \times 15 = 60$ $= x(5x + 4) + 3(5x + 4)$
$r + s = 4 + 15 = 19$ $= (5x + 4)(x + 3)$

5. $ac = -60, b = -17$ $12x^2 + 3x - 20x - 5$
$rs = 3 \times -20 = -60$ $= 3x(4x + 1) - 5(4x + 1)$
$r + s = 3 + -20 = -17$ $= (4x + 1)(3x - 5)$

Quiz 99

1. $x^2 + 2 \cdot x \cdot 3 + 3^2$
$= (x + 3)^2$

2. $x^2 - 6^2$
$= (x + 6)(x - 6)$

3. $x^2 - 2 \cdot x \cdot 7 + 7^2$
$= (x - 7)^2$

4. $(3x)^2 - 2^2$
$= (3x + 2)(3x - 2)$

5. $(2x)^2 + 2 \cdot 2x \cdot 5 + 5^2$
$= (2x + 5)^2$

Quiz 100

1. $(x - 2)(x + 7)$

2. $(2x + 3)(x - 3)$

3. $5(x^2 - 2x + 1)$
$= 5(x - 1)^2$

4. $-(4x^2 - 49)$
$= -(2x + 7)(2x - 7)$

5. $-3(x^2 - 2x - 15)$
$= -3(x + 3)(x - 5)$

Quiz 101

1. $-3(2x^2 + 3x - 20)$
$= -3(2x - 5)(x + 4)$

2. $(x^2 + 4)(x^2 - 4)$
$= (x^2 + 4)(x + 2)(x - 2)$

3. $(5x - 1)(4x + 3)$

4. $5x(x^2 + 4x + 4)$
$= 5x(x + 2)^2$

5. $2(x^3 + 2x^2 - 16x - 32)$
$= 2[x^2(x + 2) - 16(x + 2)]$
$= 2(x + 2)(x^2 - 16)$
$= 2(x + 2)(x + 4)(x - 4)$

Quiz 102

1. $(x+2)(x+5)$ **2.** $(3x+1)(4x-3)$

3. $-2x(x^2-25)$
$= -2x(x+5)(x-5)$

4. $x^2(4x+1)-4(4x+1)$
$= (4x+1)(x^2-4)$
$= (4x+1)(x+2)(x-2)$

5. $x^2(9x^2+6x+1)$
$= x^2(3x+1)^2$

Quiz 103

1. $x = \pm\sqrt{75}$
$x = \pm 5\sqrt{3}$

2. $x^2 = 16$
$x = \pm 4$

3. $x^2 = 24$
$x = \pm\sqrt{24}$
$x = \pm 2\sqrt{6}$

4. $4x^2 = 121$
$x^2 = 121/4$
$x = \pm 11/2$

5. $-3x^2 = -15$
$x^2 = 5$
$x = \pm\sqrt{5}$

Quiz 104

1. $5x^2 = 100$
$x^2 = 20$
$x = \pm\sqrt{20}$
$x = \pm 2\sqrt{5}$

2. $x+2 = \pm\sqrt{81}$
$x+2 = \pm 9$
$x = -2 \pm 9$
$x = 7, x = -11$

3. $(x-5)^2 = 54$
$x-5 = \pm\sqrt{54}$
$x-5 = \pm 3\sqrt{6}$
$x = 5 \pm 3\sqrt{6}$

4. $(x-1)^2 = 4$
$x-1 = \pm 2$
$x = 1 \pm 2$
$x = 3, x = -1$

5. $3(x+4)^2 = 33$
$(x+4)^2 = 11$
$x+4 = \pm\sqrt{11}$
$x = -4 \pm\sqrt{11}$

Quiz 105

1. $(x+2)(x+5) = 0$
$x = -2, x = -5$

2. $(x+5)(x-5) = 0$
$x = -5, x = 5$

3. $x^2 - 2x - 24 = 0$
$(x+4)(x-6) = 0$
$x = -4, x = 6$

4. $x^2 + 4x - 45 = 0$
$(x-5)(x+9) = 0$
$x = 5, x = -9$

5. $x^2 - x - 6 = 0$
$(x+2)(x-3) = 0$
$x = -2, x = 3$

Quiz 106

1. $(4x-3)(x+1) = 0$
$x = 3/4, x = -1$

2. $(3x+2)(3x-2) = 0$
$x = -2/3, x = 2/3$

3. $2x^2 - 12x + 18 = 0$
$2(x^2 - 6x + 9) = 0$
$2(x-3)^2 = 0$
$x = 3$

4. $x^2 + 4x - 5 = 0$
$(x-1)(x+5) = 0$
$x = 1, x = -5$

5. $x^2 - 7x + 12 = 0$
$(x-3)(x-4) = 0$
$x = 3, x = 4$

Quiz 107

1. $x^2 + 2x + 1 = 2 + 1$
$(x+1)^2 = 3$
$x+1 = \pm\sqrt{3}$
$x = -1 \pm\sqrt{3}$

2. $x^2 - 6x + 9 = 3 + 9$
$(x-3)^2 = 12$
$x-3 = \pm\sqrt{12}$
$x = 3 \pm 2\sqrt{3}$

3. $x^2 + 10x = -5$
$x^2 + 10x + 25 = 20$
$(x+5)^2 = 20$
$x+5 = \pm\sqrt{20}$
$x = -5 \pm 2\sqrt{5}$

4. $x^2 - 4x = -1$
$x^2 - 4x + 4 = 3$
$(x-2)^2 = 3$
$x-2 = \pm\sqrt{3}$
$x = 2 \pm\sqrt{3}$

5. $x^2 + 2x = 3$
$x^2 + 2x + 1 = 4$
$(x+1)^2 = 4$
$x+1 = \pm 2$
$x = -1 \pm 2$
$x = 1, x = -3$

Quiz 108

1. $x^2 + 4x + 4 = 1 + 4$
$(x+2)^2 = 5$
$x+2 = \pm\sqrt{5}$
$x = -2 \pm\sqrt{5}$

2. $x^2 + \dfrac{4}{3}x = \dfrac{4}{3}$
$x^2 + \dfrac{4}{3}x + \dfrac{4}{9} = \dfrac{4}{3} + \dfrac{4}{9}$
$\left(x + \dfrac{2}{3}\right)^2 = \dfrac{19}{6}$
$x + \dfrac{2}{3} = \pm\dfrac{4}{3}$
$x = -\dfrac{2}{3} \pm \dfrac{4}{3}$
$x = \dfrac{2}{3}, x = -2$

3. $x^2 + 6x - 5 = 0$
$x^2 + 6x = 5$
$x^2 + 6x + 9 = 5 + 9$
$(x+3)^2 = 14$
$x+3 = \pm\sqrt{14}$
$x = -3 \pm\sqrt{14}$

4. $5x^2 - 6x = 11$
$x^2 - \dfrac{6}{5}x = \dfrac{11}{5}$
$x^2 - \dfrac{6}{5}x + \dfrac{9}{25} = \dfrac{11}{5} + \dfrac{9}{25}$
$\left(x - \dfrac{3}{5}\right)^2 = \dfrac{64}{25}$
$x - \dfrac{3}{5} = \pm\dfrac{8}{5}$
$x = \dfrac{3}{5} \pm \dfrac{8}{5}$
$x = \dfrac{11}{5}, x = -1$

5. $3x^2 - 12x = -3$
$x^2 - 4x = -1$
$x^2 - 4x + 4 = -1 + 4$
$(x-2)^2 = 3$
$x-2 = \pm\sqrt{3}$
$x = 2 \pm\sqrt{3}$

Quiz 109

1. $a = 1, b = 0, c = -8$

$$x = \frac{-0 \pm \sqrt{0^2 - 4(1)(-8)}}{2(1)} = \frac{\pm\sqrt{32}}{2} = \pm 2\sqrt{2}$$

2. $a = 1, b = 4, c = 3$

$$x = \frac{-4 \pm \sqrt{4^2 - 4(1)(3)}}{2(1)} = \frac{-4 \pm \sqrt{4}}{2} = \frac{-4 \pm 2}{2}$$

$$x = -1, x = -3$$

3. $a = 2, b = -7, c = 4$

$$x = \frac{-(-7) \pm \sqrt{(-7)^2 - 4(2)(4)}}{2(2)} = \frac{7 \pm \sqrt{17}}{4}$$

4. $a = 5, b = 2, c = -1$

$$x = \frac{-2 \pm \sqrt{2^2 - 4(5)(-1)}}{2(5)} = \frac{-2 \pm \sqrt{24}}{10} = \frac{-1 \pm \sqrt{6}}{5}$$

5. $a = 9, b = -12, c = 4$

$$x = \frac{-(-12) \pm \sqrt{(-12)^2 - 4(9)(4)}}{2(9)} = \frac{12 \pm \sqrt{0}}{18} = \frac{2}{3}$$

Quiz 110

1. $a = 4, b = -8, c = 3$

$$x = \frac{-(-8) \pm \sqrt{(-8)^2 - 4(4)(3)}}{2(4)} = \frac{8 \pm \sqrt{16}}{8} = \frac{8 \pm 4}{8}$$

$$x = 3/2, x = 1/2$$

2. Divide both sides by 6 to simplify.
$x^2 - 9 = 0$; $a = 1, b = 0, c = -9$

$$x = \frac{-0 \pm \sqrt{0^2 - 4(1)(-9)}}{2(1)} = \frac{\pm\sqrt{36}}{2} = \frac{\pm 6}{2} = \pm 3$$

3. $x^2 - 8x + 5 = 0$; $a = 1, b = -8, c = 5$

$$x = \frac{-(-8) \pm \sqrt{(-8)^2 - 4(1)(5)}}{2(1)} = \frac{8 \pm \sqrt{44}}{2}$$

$$= 4 \pm \sqrt{11}$$

4. $5x^2 + 10x + 4 = 0$; $a = 5, b = 10, c = 4$

$$x = \frac{-10 \pm \sqrt{10^2 - 4(5)(4)}}{2(5)} = \frac{-10 \pm \sqrt{20}}{10}$$

$$= \frac{-5 \pm \sqrt{5}}{5}$$

5. $2x^2 - 7x + 2 = 0$; $a = 2, b = -7, c = 2$

$$x = \frac{-(-7) \pm \sqrt{(-7)^2 - 4(2)(2)}}{2(2)} = \frac{7 \pm \sqrt{33}}{4}$$

Quiz 111

1. By taking square roots:
$(x - 3)^2 = 25$
$x - 3 = \pm 5$
$x = 3 \pm 5$
$x = 8, x = -2$

2. By factoring:
$(x - 2)(x + 5) = 0$
$x = 2, x = -5$

3. By comp. the square:
$2x^2 + 4x = 8$
$x^2 + 2x = 4$
$x^2 + 2x + 1 = 4 + 1$
$(x + 1)^2 = 5$
$x + 1 = \pm\sqrt{5}$
$x = -1 \pm \sqrt{5}$

4. By the quad. formula:
$a = 1, b = 5, c = 3$

$$x = \frac{-5 \pm \sqrt{13}}{2}$$

5. By the quad. formula:
$a = 3, b = 6, c = 2$

$$x = \frac{-3 \pm \sqrt{3}}{3}$$

Quiz 112

1. $D = (-6)^2 - 4(1)(9) = 0$ ⇨ One solution

2. $D = (-5)^2 - 4(1)(7) = -3 < 0$ ⇨ No solution

3. $D = 5^2 - 4(2)(-2) = 41 > 0$ ⇨ Two solutions

4. By the quad. formula:
$a = 1, b = -8, c = 5$
$x = 4 \pm \sqrt{11}$

5. By factoring:
$(2x + 1)(x + 4) = 0$
$x = -1/2, x = 4$

Quiz 113

1. x = the first integer; $9 - x$ = the second integer
The sum of their squares = 53, so $x^2 + (9 - x)^2 = 53$.
$2x^2 - 18x + 28 = 0$; $2(x - 2)(x - 7) = 0$; $x = 2, x = 7$
The two positive integers are 2 and 7.

2. x = the smaller integer; $x + 4$ = the larger integer
The larger + the square of the smaller = 24,
so $(x + 4) + x^2 = 24$.
$x^2 + x - 20 = 0$; $(x - 4)(x + 5) = 0$; $x = 4, x = -5$
The two positive integers are 4 and 8.

3. x = the base of the triangle = the height of the triangle
The Pythagorean Theorem gives $x^2 + x^2 = 2^2$.
$2x^2 = 4$; $x^2 = 2$; $x = \sqrt{2}, x = -\sqrt{2}$
The perimeter is $\sqrt{2} + \sqrt{2} + 2 = 2 + 2\sqrt{2}$ feet.

4. x = the width of the strip
$8 - x$ and $7 - x$ = the dimensions of the new rectangle
The new area = the original area − 36,
so $(8 - x)(7 - x) = 8 \times 7 - 36$.
$x^2 - 15x + 36 = 0$; $(x - 3)(x - 12) = 0$; $x = 3, x = 12$
The width of the strip is 3 cm.

5. x = the distance traveled by car B

$x + 14$ = the distance traveled by car A

$x + 16$ = the distance between the two cars

The Pythagorean Theorem gives

$x^2 + (x + 14)^2 = (x + 16)^2$.

$x^2 - 4x - 60 = 0$

$(x + 6)(x - 10) = 0$

$x = -6, x = 10$

Car B traveled 10 miles. Car A traveled 24 miles. The two cars are 26 miles apart.

Quiz 114

1. By taking square roots:

$2(x + 4)^2 = 16$

$(x + 4)^2 = 8$

$x + 4 = \pm\sqrt{8}$

$x = -4 \pm 2\sqrt{2}$

2. By factoring:

$(x + 4)(x + 6) = 0$

$x = -4, x = -6$

3. By factoring:

$5(x^2 - 4x + 4) = 0$

$5(x - 2)^2 = 0$

$x = 2$

4. By the quad. formula:

$a = 2, b = 1, c = -2$

$x = \dfrac{-1 \pm \sqrt{17}}{4}$

5. Legs = x and $x - 4$, hypotenuse = $x + 4$

The Pythagorean Theorem gives $x^2 + (x - 4)^2 = (x + 4)^2$.

$x^2 - 16x = 0$; $x = 0, x = 16$

The dimensions are 12 cm, 16 cm, and 20 cm.

Quiz 115

1.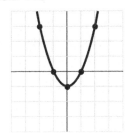

2.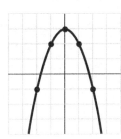

3.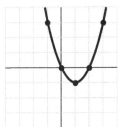

4.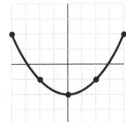

5.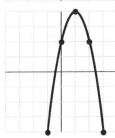

Quiz 116

1. $x = -\dfrac{8}{2(1)} = -4$

$y = -7$ at $x = -4$

Vertex: $(-4, -7)$

2. $x = -\dfrac{6}{2(-1)} = 3$

$y = 8$ at $x = 3$

Vertex: $(3, 8)$

3.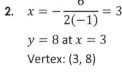

4.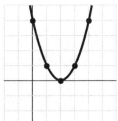

5.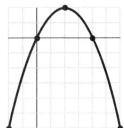

Quiz 117

1. $h = 5, k = 3$

Vertex: $(5, 3)$

2. $h = -2, k = -9$

Vertex: $(-2, -9)$

3.

4.

5.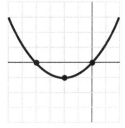

Quiz 118

1. x-intercepts: $-3, 3$

Find the vertex:

$x = (-3 + 3)/2 = 0$

$y = -9$ at $x = 0$

Vertex: $(0, -9)$

2. x-intercepts: $3, 9$

Find the vertex:

$x = (3 + 9)/2 = 6$

$y = 6$ at $x = 6$

Vertex: $(6, 6)$

3.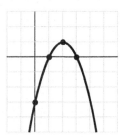

4.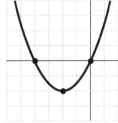

5.

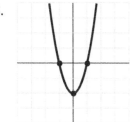

Quiz 119

1. $y = x^2 + 6x + \mathbf{9 - 9} + 5$
   $= (x + 3)^2 - 4$

2. $y = -2(x^2 - 4x + \mathbf{4 - 4}) - 1$
   $= -2(x^2 - 4x + 4) + 8 - 1$
   $= -2(x - 2)^2 + 7$

3. $y = (x + 2)(x - 4)$

4. $y = \frac{1}{2}(x^2 + 6x) = \frac{1}{2}x(x + 6)$

5.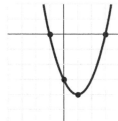

Quiz 120

1. $y = -4(x - 1)^2$ Vertex: (1, 0)
   $= -4x^2 + 8x - 4$ x-intercept(s): 1
                               y-intercept: −4

2. $y = \frac{1}{3}(x + 1)(x - 5)$ x-intercepts: −1, 5
                               Vertex: (2, −3)
   $= \frac{1}{3}x^2 - \frac{4}{3}x - \frac{5}{3}$ x = (−1 + 5)/2 = 2
                               y = −3 at x = 2
                               y-intercept: −5/3

3. $y = -x^2 - 4x + 5$ y-intercept: 5
   $= -(x^2 + 4x - 5)$
   $= -(x - 1)(x + 5)$ x-intercepts: 1, −5
   $y = -(x^2 + 4x + \mathbf{4 - 4}) + 5$
   $= -(x^2 + 4x + 4) + 4 + 5$
   $= -(x + 2)^2 + 9$ Vertex: (−2, 9)

4. $y = 2x^2 - 8$ y-intercept: −8
   $= 2(x - 0)^2 - 8$ Vertex: (0, −8)
   $y = 2(x^2 - 4)$
   $= 2(x + 2)(x - 2)$ x-intercepts: −2, 2

5. $y = -x^2 + 6x - 5$ y-intercept: −5
   $= -(x^2 - 6x + 5)$
   $= -(x - 1)(x - 5)$ x-intercepts: 1, 5
   $y = -(x^2 - 6x + \mathbf{9 - 9}) - 5$
   $= -(x^2 - 6x + 9) + 9 - 5$
   $= -(x - 3)^2 + 4$ Vertex: (3, 4)

Quiz 121

1. Vertex form: $y = a(x - 1)^2 + 3$
   Plug in (0, 2): $2 = a(0 - 1)^2 + 3$
   Solve for a: $2 = a + 3; a = -1$
   Vertex form: $y = -(x - 1)^2 + 3$
   Standard form: $y = -x^2 + 2x + 2$

2. $y = a(x - 5)^2 + 3$ 3. $y = a(x + 3)^2$
   $-6 = a(2 - 5)^2 + 3$ $8 = a(-1 + 3)^2$
   $-6 = 9a + 3; a = -1$ $8 = 4a; a = 2$
   $y = -(x - 5)^2 + 3$ $y = 2(x + 3)^2$
   $y = -x^2 + 10x - 22$ $y = 2x^2 + 12x + 18$

4. $y = a(x + 2)(x - 1)$ 5. $y = ax(x - 8)$
   $-6 = a(0 + 2)(0 - 1)$ $5 = a(-2)(-2 - 8)$
   $-6 = -2a; a = 3$ $5 = 20a; a = 1/4$
   $y = 3(x + 2)(x - 1)$
   $y = 3x^2 + 3x - 6$ $y = \frac{1}{4}x(x - 8)$

                                      $y = \frac{1}{4}x^2 - 2x$

Quiz 122

1. There is no scaling or flipping, so a = 1.
   The vertex is at (3, 0) after shifting, so h = 3 and k = 0.
   $y = (x - 3)^2$

2. $y = -x^2 + 2$ 3. $y = (x + 2)^2 - 5$

4. $y = 3(x - 4)^2 + 2$ 5. $y = -2(x + 1)^2$

Quiz 123

1. $h(t) = -16(t - 4)^2 + 256$
   It reaches the maximum height after 4 seconds.

2. $h(t) = -16(t + 3)(t - 3)$
   It will hit the ground after 3 seconds.

3. $-16t^2 + 64t + 80 = 80$
   $-16t^2 + 64t = 0; -16t(t - 4) = 0; t = 0, t = 4$
   It will be at a height of 80 feet again after 4 seconds.

4. $h(t) = -16(t - 1)^2 + 256$
   The maximum height is 256 feet.

5. $c(x) = 0.2(x - 20)^2 + 10$
   The cost is minimized when 20 parts are produced.

Quiz 124

1.

$y = x^2 - 2x + \mathbf{1} - \mathbf{1} + 2$
$y = (x - 1)^2 + 1$

Vertex: (1, 1)
y-intercept: 2

2.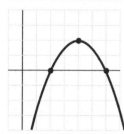

$y = -\dfrac{1}{2}(x^2 - 8x + 12)$

$y = -\dfrac{1}{2}(x - 2)(x - 6)$

x-intercept: 2, 6
Vertex: (4, 2)

3. Find the function:

$y = a(x - 2)(x - 6)$
$-5 = a(7 - 2)(7 - 6)$
$-5 = 5a; \ a = -1$
$y = -(x - 2)(x - 6)$

Find the vertex:

$x = (2 + 6)/2 = 4$
$y = 4$ at $x = 4$
Vertex: (4, 4)

4. The graph is scaled by 3 and flipped, so $a = -3$.
The vertex is at (0, 4) after shifting, so $h = 0$ and $k = 4$.
$y = -3x^2 + 4$

5. $h(t) = -16(t - 3)^2 + 400$
It reaches the maximum height after 3 seconds.

Quiz 125

1. $\dfrac{x}{7}$ $for \ x \neq 0$

2. $\dfrac{(x + 2)(x - 2)}{x(x + 2)} = \dfrac{x - 2}{x}$ $for \ x \neq 0, -2$

3. $\dfrac{x + 7}{(x - 2)(x + 7)} = \dfrac{1}{x - 2}$ $for \ x \neq 2, -7$

4. $\dfrac{(x - 3)^2}{(2x + 1)(x - 3)} = \dfrac{x - 3}{2x + 1}$ $for \ x \neq -\dfrac{1}{2}, 3$

5. $\dfrac{x(x + 1)(x + 4)}{(x + 4)(x + 1)(x - 1)} = \dfrac{x}{x - 1}$ $for \ x \neq -4, -1, 1$

Quiz 126

1. $\dfrac{2}{3x}$ $for \ x \neq 0$

2. $\dfrac{x^2 + 3x}{x + 5} \cdot \dfrac{2x + 10}{x + 3} = \dfrac{x(x + 3)}{x + 5} \cdot \dfrac{2(x + 5)}{x + 3} = 2x$

$for \ x \neq -5, -3$

3. $\dfrac{(x - 2)^2}{3x(x - 2)} \cdot \dfrac{x^2}{x - 2} = \dfrac{x}{3}$ $for \ x \neq 0, 2$

4. $\dfrac{(x - 3)(x + 5)}{x(2x + 3)} \cdot \dfrac{2x + 3}{x + 5} = \dfrac{x - 3}{x}$ $for \ x \neq 0, -\dfrac{3}{2}, -5$

5. $\dfrac{2x^2 - 3x - 20}{4x^3 - 25x} \cdot \dfrac{x^2}{x^2 - 4x}$

$= \dfrac{(2x + 5)(x - 4)}{x(2x + 5)(2x - 5)} \cdot \dfrac{x^2}{x(x - 4)} = \dfrac{1}{2x - 5}$

$for \ x \neq 0, -\dfrac{5}{2}, \dfrac{5}{2}, 4$

Quiz 127

1. $\dfrac{x^2 + 9 + 6x}{x + 3} = \dfrac{(x + 3)^2}{x + 3} = x + 3$ $for \ x \neq -3$

2. $\dfrac{(x + 2)(x + 3)}{x(x + 3)} - \dfrac{(x + 5)x}{(x + 3)x} = \dfrac{6}{x(x + 3)}$ $for \ x \neq 0, -3$

3. $\dfrac{x - 2}{x^2 - 4} = \dfrac{x - 2}{(x + 2)(x - 2)} = \dfrac{1}{x + 2}$ $for \ x \neq -2, 2$

4. $\dfrac{x + 2}{x - 3} - \dfrac{x - 2}{(x - 2)(x - 3)} = \dfrac{x + 2}{x - 3} - \dfrac{1}{x - 3} = \dfrac{x + 1}{x - 3}$

$for \ x \neq 3, 2$

5. $\dfrac{3x + 9}{(2x + 1)(x + 3)} + \dfrac{x}{2x + 1}$

$= \dfrac{3x + 9}{(2x + 1)(x + 3)} + \dfrac{x(x + 3)}{(2x + 1)(x + 3)}$

$= \dfrac{x^2 + 6x + 9}{(2x + 1)(x + 3)} = \dfrac{(x + 3)^2}{(2x + 1)(x + 3)} = \dfrac{x + 3}{2x + 1}$

$for \ x \neq -\dfrac{1}{2}, -3$

Quiz 128

1. Excluded: $x \neq 0$; LCD $= 2x$
Multiply both sides by the LCD, then solve for x.
$x - 6 = 1$
$x = 7$

2. Excluded: $x \neq -4, -5$; LCD $= (x + 4)(x + 5)$
Multiply both sides by the LCD, then solve for x.
$2(x + 5) = 3(x + 4)$ $\Rightarrow$ $x = -2$
$2x + 10 = 3x + 12$

3. Excluded: $x \neq -4, 0$; LCD $= x(x + 4)$
Multiply both sides by the LCD, then solve for x.
$x^2 - (x + 4) = x + 4$ $\Rightarrow$ $(x + 2)(x - 4) = 0$
$x^2 - 2x - 8 = 0$ $\qquad x = -2, x = 4$

4. Excluded: $x \neq -3, 0$; LCD $= x(x + 3)$
   Multiply both sides by the LCD, then solve for x.
   $x^2 = x + 3 - 3x$ $x = 1, x = -3$
   $x^2 + 2x - 3 = 0$ Exclude -3.
   $(x - 1)(x + 3) = 0$ $x = 1$

5. $\dfrac{3}{x} - \dfrac{1}{x + 2} = \dfrac{x - 2}{x(x + 2)}$

   Excluded: $x \neq 0, -2$; LCD $= x(x + 2)$
   Multiply both sides by the LCD, then solve for x.
   $3(x + 2) - x = x - 2$ $x = -8$
   $2x + 6 = x - 2$

Quiz 129

1. Excluded: $x \neq 0$; LCD $= 4x$
   Multiply both sides by the LCD, then solve for x.
   $x^2 + 12 = 4(x + 2)$ $(x - 2)^2 = 0$
   $x^2 - 4x + 4 = 0$ $x = 2$

2. Excluded: $x \neq 0$; LCD $= 6x^2$
   Multiply both sides by the LCD, then solve for x.
   $2x - 3(x + 1) = 6(x - 4)$ $x = 3$
   $-x - 3 = 6x - 24$

3. Excluded: $x \neq -3/2, -1/2$; LCD $= (2x + 3)(2x + 1)$
   Multiply both sides by the LCD, then solve for x.
   $(x + 1)(2x + 1) = x(2x + 3)$
   $2x^2 + 3x + 1 = 2x^2 + 3x$ $1 = 0$
   $0x^2 + 0x + 1 = 0$ No solution

4. Excluded: $x \neq 1/3, 1$; LCD $= (3x - 1)(x - 1)$
   Multiply both sides by the LCD, then solve for x.
   $x(x - 1) + 3x - 1 = x - 1$
   $x^2 + x = 0$ $x = 0, x = -1$
   $x(x + 1) = 0$

5. $\dfrac{x}{x - 2} - \dfrac{2}{x + 3} = \dfrac{10}{(x - 2)(x + 3)}$

   Excluded: $x \neq 2, -3$; LCD $= (x - 2)(x + 3)$
   Multiply both sides by the LCD, then solve for x.
   $x(x + 3) - 2(x - 2) = 10$ $x = 2, x = -3$
   $x^2 + x - 6 = 0$ Exclude 2 and -3.
   $(x - 2)(x + 3) = 0$ No solution

Quiz 130

1. x = time together
   $\dfrac{1}{3} + \dfrac{1}{6} = \dfrac{1}{x}$
   LCD $= 6x$; $x = 2$
   It will take 2 hours.

2. x = time together
   $\dfrac{1}{20} + \dfrac{1}{30} = \dfrac{1}{x}$
   LCD $= 60x$; $x = 12$
   It will take 12 minutes.

3. x = Mark's time alone
   $\dfrac{1}{5} + \dfrac{1}{x} = \dfrac{1}{3}$
   LCD $= 15x$; $x = 7.5$
   It will take 7.5 hours.

4. x = time together
   $\dfrac{1}{2} + \dfrac{1}{3} + \dfrac{1}{6} = \dfrac{1}{x}$
   LCD $= 6x$; $x = 1$
   It will take 1 hour.

5. x = Pipe A's time alone
   $4x$ = Pipe B's time alone
   $\dfrac{1}{x} + \dfrac{1}{4x} = \dfrac{1}{4}$
   LCD $= 4x$; $x = 5$
   It will take 5 hours.

Quiz 131

1. $\dfrac{x(x - 2)(x + 5)}{(x + 5)(x + 2)(x - 2)} = \dfrac{x}{x + 2}$ $for\ x \neq -5, -2, 2$

2. $\dfrac{x^2 - 4x - 12}{3x + 4} \cdot \dfrac{3x^2 + 4x}{x + 2}$

   $= \dfrac{(x + 2)(x - 6)}{3x + 4} \cdot \dfrac{x(3x + 4)}{x + 2} = x(x - 6)$

   $for\ x \neq -\dfrac{4}{3}, 0, -2$

3. $\dfrac{x^2 - 11}{(x + 2)(x - 5)} - \dfrac{2(x + 2)}{(x - 5)(x + 2)} = \dfrac{x^2 - 2x - 15}{(x + 2)(x - 5)}$

   $= \dfrac{(x + 3)(x - 5)}{(x + 2)(x - 5)} = \dfrac{x + 3}{x + 2}$ $for\ x \neq -2, 5$

4. Excluded: $x \neq 0, -4$; LCD $= x(x + 4)$
   Multiply both sides by the LCD, then solve for x.
   $x + 4 - x^2 = 4$ $x = 0, x = 1$
   $x^2 - x = 0$ Exclude 0.
   $x(x - 1) = 0$ $x = 1$

5. x = time together
   $\dfrac{1}{9} + \dfrac{1}{6} = \dfrac{1}{x}$
   LCD $= 18x$; $x = 18/5 = 3.6$
   It will take 3.6 hours.

Quiz 138

1. Mean = 5   Median = 5   Mode(s) = 3

2. Mean = 6   Median = 6.5   Mode(s) = 9

3. Mean = 18   Median = 16.5   Mode(s) = 15

4. Mean = $(4 + 5 + 9 + x + 2 + 8)/6 = 6$
   Solve for x, and you get $x = 8$.

5. Mean = $(3 + x + 6 + 2 + 7 + 3 + 9)/7 = 5$
   Solve for x, and you get $x = 5$.

Quiz 139

1. Range = 6   S. deviation = 2.3   (Mean = 4)
2. Range = 3   S. deviation = 1.1   (Mean = 5)
3. Range = 0   S. deviation = 0   (Mean = 3)
4. Range = 6   S. deviation = 2   (Mean = 4)
5. Range = 5   S. deviation = 1.6   (Mean = 5)

Quiz 140

1. Min = 2   Q1 = 3   Q2 = 6   Q3 = 8   Max = 9
2. Min = 2   Q1 = 4   Q2 = 5   Q3 = 6.5   Max = 8
3. Median = 90   4. Range = 35   5. 25%

Quiz 141

1. Median = 17   2. 20 children   3. 5 games
4. 3 goals   5. 230 children

Quiz 142

1. Symmetric   2. Skewed left
3. Skewed right   4. Mean
5. Interquartile range

Quiz 143

1. Positive correlation   2. Negative correlation
3. Negative correlation   4. No correlation
5. D) $y = -x + 5$

Quiz 144

1. 200 customers   2. 46 + 54 = 100 customers
3. 52/200 = 26%   4. 54/200 = 27%
5. 52/(52+48) = 52%

Quiz 145

1. Mean = 5   Median = 5.5   Mode(s) = 6
2. Median = 10   IQR = 3
3. Skewed right   4. D) Mean and IQR
5. 48/200 = 24%

Quiz 146

1. Possible: 20 balls
   Favorable: 5 white balls
   P = 5/20 = 1/4
2. Possible: 1 to 6
   Favorable: 1 to 6
   P = 6/6 = 1
3. Possible: 1 to 10
   Favorable: 3, 6, 9
   P = 3/10
4. Total tries: 30
   Hits: 14
   P = 14/30 = 7/15
5. Total tries: 27
   Misses: 27 − 18 = 9
   P = 9/27 = 1/3

Quiz 147

1. 8   2. 365   3. 2 × 26 = 52
4. 5 × 6 × 2 = 60   5. 6 × 4 = 24

Quiz 148

1. 2 × 2 × 2 × 2 = 16   2. 6 × 2 × 2 = 24
3. 4 × 4 × 4 = 64   4. 5 × 5 × 5 = 125
5. 5 × 4 × 3 = 60

Quiz 149

1. P(heads and heads)
   = P(heads) × P(heads)
   $= \dfrac{1}{2} \times \dfrac{1}{2} = \dfrac{1}{4}$
2. P(5 and odd)
   = P(5) × P(odd)
   $= \dfrac{1}{6} \times \dfrac{1}{2} = \dfrac{1}{12}$
3. P(both > 4)
   = P(1st > 4) × P(2nd > 4)
   $= \dfrac{1}{3} \times \dfrac{1}{3} = \dfrac{1}{9}$
4. P(odd and even)
   = P(odd) × P(even)
   $= \dfrac{3}{5} \times \dfrac{2}{5} = \dfrac{6}{25}$
5. P(yellow and yellow)
   = P(yellow) × P(yellow)
   $= \dfrac{2}{10} \times \dfrac{2}{10} = \dfrac{1}{25}$

Quiz 150

1. P(odd and odd)
   = P(odd) × P(odd | odd)
   $= \dfrac{3}{5} \times \dfrac{2}{4} = \dfrac{3}{10}$
2. P(red and red)
   = P(red) × P(red | red)
   $= \dfrac{3}{10} \times \dfrac{2}{9} = \dfrac{1}{15}$
3. P(5 and 5) = P(5) × P(5 | 5)
   $= \dfrac{1}{9} \times \dfrac{0}{8} = 0$
4. P = 5/25 = 1/5
   5 × 5 = 25 possible outcomes
   5 favorable outcomes: 11, 22, 33, 44, 55
5. P = 4/36 = 1/9
   6 × 6 = 36 possible outcomes
   4 favorable outcomes: 36, 45, 54, 63

Quiz 151

1. $P(2 \text{ or odd}) = P(2) + P(\text{odd})$

   $= \dfrac{1}{6} + \dfrac{1}{2} = \dfrac{2}{3}$

2. $P(2 \text{ or prime}) = P(2) + P(\text{prime}) - P(2 \text{ and prime})$

   $= \dfrac{1}{6} + \dfrac{1}{2} - \dfrac{1}{6} = \dfrac{1}{2}$

3. $P(\text{greater than 3 or odd}) = P(\text{greater than 3}) + P(\text{odd}) -$
   $P(\text{greater than 3 and odd})$

   $= \dfrac{1}{2} + \dfrac{1}{2} - \dfrac{1}{6} = \dfrac{5}{6}$

4. $P(\text{ace or face}) = P(\text{ace}) + P(\text{face})$

   $= \dfrac{4}{52} + \dfrac{12}{52} = \dfrac{4}{13}$

5. $P(\text{black or face}) = P(\text{black}) + P(\text{face}) - P(\text{black and face})$

   $= \dfrac{26}{52} + \dfrac{12}{52} - \dfrac{6}{52} = \dfrac{8}{13}$

Quiz 152

1. $5 \times 4 \times 3 \times 2 \times 1 = 120$ 2. $(5 \times 4 \times 3)/(3 \times 2 \times 1) = 10$

3. $10 \times 9 \times 8 = 720$ 4. $5 \times 4 \times 3 = 60$

5. $(52 \times 51)/(2 \times 1) = 1{,}326$

Quiz 153

1. $C(8, 3) = \dfrac{8!}{(8-3)!\,3!} = \dfrac{8 \times 7 \times 6 \times 5!}{5!\,3!} = 56$

2. $P(4, 4) = \dfrac{4!}{(4-4)!} = 4! = 24$

3. $P(7, 3) = \dfrac{7!}{(7-3)!} = \dfrac{7!}{4!} = \dfrac{7 \times 6 \times 5 \times 4!}{4!} = 210$

4. $C(9, 4) = \dfrac{9!}{(9-4)!\,4!} = \dfrac{9 \times 8 \times 7 \times 6 \times 5!}{5!\,4!} = 126$

5. $C(20, 2) = \dfrac{20!}{(20-2)!\,2!} = \dfrac{20 \times 19 \times 18!}{18!\,2!} = 190$

Quiz 154

1. Total possible outcomes = $P(5, 5)$
   Favorable outcomes = 1

   Probability $= \dfrac{1}{P(5, 5)} = \dfrac{1}{120}$

2. Favorable outcomes = permutations of 4 remaining
   letters after placing E as the first letter + permutations
   of 4 remaining letters after placing I as the first letter
   $= P(4, 4) + P(4, 4) = 2 \times P(4, 4)$

   Probability $= \dfrac{2 \times P(4, 4)}{P(5, 5)} = \dfrac{2 \times 24}{120} = \dfrac{2}{5}$

3. Favorable outcomes = E first and I last + I first and E last
   $= P(3, 3) + P(3, 3) = 2 \times P(3, 3)$

   Probability $= \dfrac{2 \times P(3, 3)}{P(5, 5)} = \dfrac{2 \times 6}{120} = \dfrac{1}{10}$

4. Total possible outcomes = $C(9, 2)$
   Favorable outcomes = combinations of choosing 2 balls
   from 4 yellow balls = $C(4, 2)$

   Probability $= \dfrac{C(4, 2)}{C(9, 2)} = \dfrac{6}{36} = \dfrac{1}{6}$

5. Favorable outcomes = combinations of choosing 2 balls
   from 4 yellow and 3 white balls = $C(7, 2)$

   Probability $= \dfrac{C(7, 2)}{C(9, 2)} = \dfrac{21}{36} = \dfrac{7}{12}$

Quiz 155

1. $P = 2 \text{ white balls} / 10 \text{ balls} = 1/5$

2. $P(\text{three tails}) = P(\text{tails}) \times P(\text{tails}) \times P(\text{tails})$

   $= \dfrac{1}{2} \times \dfrac{1}{2} \times \dfrac{1}{2} = \dfrac{1}{8}$

3. $P = 6/36 = 1/6$

   $6 \times 6 = 36$ possible outcomes
   6 favorable outcomes: 11, 22, 33, 44, 55, 66

4. $P(\text{prime or odd}) = P(\text{prime}) + P(\text{odd}) - P(\text{prime \& odd})$

   $= \dfrac{1}{2} + \dfrac{1}{2} - \dfrac{2}{6} = \dfrac{2}{3}$

5. Total possible outcomes = $P(5, 5)$

   Favorable outcomes = permutations of 4 remaining
   numbers after placing 2 or 4 first = $2 \times P(4, 4)$

   $P = \dfrac{2 \times P(4, 4)}{P(5, 5)} = \dfrac{2 \times 24}{120} = \dfrac{2}{5}$

Quiz 158

1. $7x - 8 = 3x + 8$ 2. $4|x - 5| = 24$
   $4x - 8 = 8$ $|x - 5| = 6$
   $4x = 16$ $x - 5 = -6$ or $x - 5 = 6$
   $x = 4$ $x = -1$ or $x = 11$

3. $-30 < -5x \leq 35$ 4. $|-6x| \geq 18$
   $-7 \leq x < 6$ $-6x \leq -18$ or $-6x \geq 18$
                           $x \geq 3$ or $x \leq -3$
                           $x \leq -3$ or $x \geq 3$

5. Let three integers be x, $x + 2$, and $x + 4$.
   $x + (x + 2) + (x + 4) = 78$; $x = 24$
   The three integers are 24, 26, and 28.

Quiz 159

1.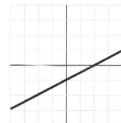

2.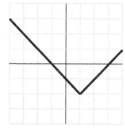

3.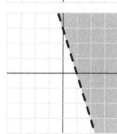

4. $m = \dfrac{-5 - 7}{2 - (-1)} = -4$

Use $(-1, 7)$ to find b:

$7 = -4(-1) + b$

$b = 3$

$y = -4x + 3$

5. The answer is **B**.

Quiz 160

1. Solve by substitution:

$4x + 5(-2x - 9) = 3$

$-6x - 45 = 3$

$x = -8$

$\Rightarrow$ $y = -2(-8) - 9 = 7$

Solution: $(-8, 7)$

2. Solve by elimination:

eq1 + eq2

$7x = 7$

$x = 1$

$\Rightarrow$ $2(1) + 3y = 8$

$y = 2$

Solution: $(1, 2)$

3. Solve by elimination:

eq1 × 2 – eq2

$x = -1$

$\Rightarrow$ $3(-1) + 2y = 7$

$y = 5$

Solution: $(-1, 5)$

4. x = speed of the plane in still air, y = speed of the wind

$6(x + y) = 1680$, $7(x - y) = 1680$

$x = 260$, $y = 20$

The speed of the airplane in still air would be 260 mph and the speed of the wind was 20 mph.

5.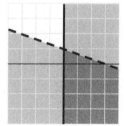

Quiz 161

1. Domain: $0 < x \le 4$

Range: $-1 \le y \le 2$

2. $f(4) = -1$, so $f^{-1}(-1) = 4$.

$f(2) + f^{-1}(-1) = 2 + 4 = 6$

3. The table is linear.

4. $k = 2 \times 8 = 16$, so $xy = 16$.

When $y = 4$, $x = 4$.

5. $a_1 = 5, d = 3$

$a_n = 5 + 3(n - 1) = 3n + 2$

Quiz 162

1. $9 \div 3 - 2 \times (-1) = 3 + 2 = 5$

2. $\sqrt{16 \cdot 5x^2yz^2} = 4xz\sqrt{5y}$

3. $3\sqrt{24} - \sqrt{18} - 2\sqrt{54} + \sqrt{32}$

$= 3\sqrt{4 \cdot 6} - \sqrt{9 \cdot 2} - 2\sqrt{9 \cdot 6} + \sqrt{16 \cdot 2}$

$= 6\sqrt{6} - 3\sqrt{2} - 6\sqrt{6} + 4\sqrt{2} = \sqrt{2}$

4. Square both sides.

$2x + 5 = x + 9$

$x = 4$

5. $x^2 + 7^2 = 14^2$

$x^2 = 147$

$x = \pm\sqrt{147} = \pm 7\sqrt{3}$

The length is 7√3 inches.

Quiz 163

1. $15x^{4-3} = 15x$

2. $x^5 \cdot 2^{-2}x^{-4} = \dfrac{x}{2^2} = \dfrac{x}{4}$

3. $(3^3x^3)^{2/3}$

$= 3^2x^2 = 9x^2$

4. $\left(2^5x^{1/4}\right)^{4/5}$

$= 2^4x^{1/5} = 16x^{1/5}$

5. Initial value $a = 200$

Growth factor $b = 1.05$

$y = 200(1.05)^x$

$\Rightarrow$ $y = 255.256 \ldots$ at $x = 5$

The coin will be worth about $255.26.

Quiz 164

1. $(x^2 - 16)(x - 2)$

$= x^3 - 2x^2 - 16x + 32$

2.

$$
\begin{array}{r}
3x - 4 \\
x + 2 \overline{\smash{\big)}\ 3x^2 + 2x - 8} \\
\underline{3x^2 + 6x} \\
-4x - 8 \\
\underline{-4x - 8} \\
0
\end{array}
$$

Answer: $3x - 4$

3. $3x^2 + x + 9x + 3$

$= x(3x + 1) + 3(3x + 1)$

$= (3x + 1)(x + 3)$

4. $8x(x^2 - 2x + 1) = 8x(x - 1)^2$

5. $-(4x^3 + 12x^2 - x - 3)$

$= -[4x^2(x + 3) - (x + 3)]$

$= -(x + 3)(4x^2 - 1)$

$= -(x + 3)(2x + 1)(2x - 1)$

Quiz 165

1. By taking square roots:
$2(x-1)^2 = 18$
$(x-1)^2 = 9$
$x - 1 = \pm 3$
$x = 1 \pm 3$
$x = 4, x = -2$

2. By factoring:
$3(x^2 - 3x + 2) = 0$
$3(x-1)(x-2) = 0$
$x = 1, x = 2$

3. By comp. the square:
$x^2 + 6x = -3$
$x^2 + 6x + 9 = -3 + 9$
$(x+3)^2 = 6$
$x + 3 = \pm\sqrt{6}$
$x = -3 \pm \sqrt{6}$

4. By the quad. formula:
$a = 4, b = 7, c = 2$
$$x = \frac{-7 \pm \sqrt{17}}{8}$$

5. x = width; $2x + 3$ = length
The area is 90, so $x(2x + 3) = 90$.
$2x^2 + 3x - 90 = 0$; $(x - 6)(2x + 15) = 0$; $x = 6$, $x = -15/2$
The dimensions are 6 cm and 15 cm.

Quiz 166

1. $y = 2x^2 - 4x$
$= 2x(x - 2)$
$= 2(x - 1)^2 - 2$

y-intercept: 0
x-intercepts: 0, 2
Vertex: (1, –2)

2. $y = -x^2 - 2x + 3$
$= -(x - 1)(x + 3)$
$= -(x + 1)^2 + 4$

y-intercept: 3
x-intercepts: 1, –3
Vertex: (–1, 4)

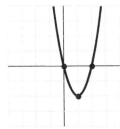
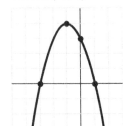

3. Find the function:
$y = a(x + 2)^2 - 8$
$10 = a(1 + 2)^2 - 8$
$10 = 9a - 8$; $a = 2$
$y = 2(x + 2)^2 - 8$

Find the zeros:
$y = 2x^2 + 8x$
$y = 2x(x + 4)$
The zeros are 0 and –4.

4. $y = -4(x + 5)^2$

5. $-16t(t - 6) = 0$
After 6 seconds

Quiz 167

1. $\dfrac{(2x + 3)(2x - 3)}{(2x - 3)(x + 4)} = \dfrac{2x + 3}{x + 4}$ for $x \neq \dfrac{3}{2}, -4$

2. $\dfrac{5x + 15}{x^2 - 10x + 25} \cdot \dfrac{x - 5}{x + 3}$

$= \dfrac{5(x + 3)}{(x - 5)^2} \cdot \dfrac{x - 5}{x + 3} = \dfrac{5}{x - 5}$ for $x \neq 5, -3$

3. $\dfrac{x(x - 4)}{(x - 3)(x - 4)} - \dfrac{x - 6}{(x - 3)(x - 4)}$

$= \dfrac{x^2 - 5x + 6}{(x - 3)(x - 4)} = \dfrac{(x - 2)(x - 3)}{(x - 3)(x - 4)} = \dfrac{x - 2}{x - 4}$

for $x \neq 3, 4$

4. Excluded: $x \neq 0, -5$; LCD $= x(x + 5)$
Multiply both sides by the LCD, then solve for x.
$x^2 = 4(x + 5) - 3x$ ⟹ $(x + 4)(x - 5) = 0$
$x^2 - x - 20 = 0$ ⟹ $x = -4, x = 5$

5. x = Leah's time alone
$$\frac{1}{60} + \frac{1}{x} = \frac{1}{15}$$
LCD $= 60x$; $x = 20$
It will take 20 minutes.

Quiz 168

1. Mean = 7   Median = 6.5   Mode(s) = 8

2. Median = 5.5   3. Skewed left

4. Positive correlation   5. 48/(32 + 48) = 60%

Quiz 169

1. $P = 3/5$
Possible: 1 to 5
Favorable: 1, 3, 5

2. P(prime and odd)
$= P$(prime) x P(odd)
$= 1/2 \times 1/2 = 1/4$

3. $P = 6/36 = 1/6$
$6 \times 6 = 36$ possible outcomes
6 favorable outcomes: 16, 25, 34, 43, 52, 61

4. P(red or face) = P(red) + P(face) – P(red and face)
$$= \frac{26}{52} + \frac{12}{52} - \frac{6}{52} = \frac{8}{13}$$

5. Total possible outcomes = $C(6, 2)$
Favorable outcomes = combinations of choosing 2 balls from 4 green balls = $C(4, 2)$
$$\text{Probability} = \frac{C(4, 2)}{C(6, 2)} = \frac{6}{15} = \frac{2}{5}$$

Quiz 170

1. $5x = -5$
$x = -1$

2. $2x - 3 = 9 - 4x$
$6x = 12$
$x = 2$

3. Multiply by 100.
$40x + 170 = 202$
$40x = 32$
$x = 4/5$

4. Multiply by 12.
$4x + 9 = 6x + 2$
$-2x = -7$
$x = 7/2$

5. $4|3 - 2x| = 12$
$|3 - 2x| = 3$
$3 - 2x = -3$ or $3 - 2x = 3$
$-2x = -6$ or $-2x = 0$
$x = 3$ or $x = 0$

Quiz 171

1. $9x \leq 36$
$x \leq 4$

2. $-2x - 4 > -8$
$-2x > -4$
$x < 2$

3. $-10 \leq -5x < 5$
$-1 < x \leq 2$

4. $4x \geq 12$ or $-x < 2$
$x \geq 3$ or $x > -2$
$x > -2$

5. Multiply by 5.
$2|x + 3| - 5 < 3$
$2|x + 3| < 8$

$\Rightarrow$ $|x + 3| < 4$
$-4 < x + 3 < 4$
$-7 < x < 1$

Quiz 172

1. $3x + (x + 3) = 15$
$x = 3$
$y = 3 + 3 = 6$
Solution: (3, 6)

2. eq1 + eq 2
$5x = -5; x = -1$
$2(-1) + y = 7; y = 9$
Solution: (-1, 9)

3. eq1 × 2 – eq 2
$0x + 0y = -15$
No solution

4. eq1 × 2 – eq 2
$9y = -18; y = -2$
$2x + 7(-2) = -4; x = 5$
Solution: (5, -2)

5. eq1 ÷ 3 – eq2 ÷ 2
$0x + 0y = 0$
Infinitely many solutions

Quiz 173

1. $4\sqrt{x} = 8$
$\sqrt{x} = 2$
$x = 4$

2. $\sqrt{x - 3} = -3 < 0$
No solution

3. $\sqrt{2x - 1} = 3$
$2x - 1 = 9$
$2x = 10$
$x = 5$

4. $3x + 8 = x + 4$
$2x = -4$
$x = -2$

5. $9(x - 1) = 6x - 7$
$9x - 9 = 6x - 7$
$3x = 2$
$x = 2/3$

Quiz 174

1. $(x + 3)(x - 6) = 0$
$x = -3, x = 6$

2. $(x - 1)^2 = 20$
$x - 1 = \pm\sqrt{20}$
$x = 1 \pm 2\sqrt{5}$

3. $a = 2, b = 4, c = 7$
$D = b^2 - 4ac$
$\quad = -10 < 0$
No solution

4. $4(x^2 - x - 6) = 0$
$4(x + 2)(x - 3) = 0$
$x = -2, x = 3$

5. $x^2 + 10x = -18$
$x^2 + 10x + 25 = -18 + 25$
$(x + 5)^2 = 7$
$x + 5 = \pm\sqrt{7}$
$x = -5 \pm \sqrt{7}$

Quiz 175

1. Excluded: $x \neq 1/4, -3$; LCD $= (4x - 1)(x + 3)$
Multiply both sides by the LCD, then solve for x.
$2(x + 3) = 3(4x - 1)$ $\Rightarrow$ $-10x = -9$
$2x + 6 = 12x - 3$ $\quad$ $x = 9/10$

2. Excluded: $x \neq 0, -1$; LCD $= 2x(x + 1)$
Multiply both sides by the LCD, then solve for x.
$4(x + 1) + 2x(x - 3) = x(x + 1)$
$x^2 - 3x + 4 = 0$ $\Rightarrow$ No solution
$D = b^2 - 4ac = -7 < 0$

3. Excluded: $x \neq 0$; LCD $= 9x$
Multiply both sides by the LCD, then solve for x.
$3(x + 2) - 9 = x - 1$ $\Rightarrow$ $2x = 2$
$3x - 3 = x - 1$ $\quad$ $x = 1$

4. Excluded: $x \neq -3, 1$; LCD $= (x + 3)(x - 1)$
Multiply both sides by the LCD, then solve for x.
$(x + 1)(x - 1) - (x + 3) = 4(x - 1)$
$x^2 - 5x = 0$ $\Rightarrow$ $x = 0, x = 5$
$x(x - 5) = 0$

5. $\dfrac{x}{x + 2} = \dfrac{x + 16}{(x + 2)(x - 5)}$
Excluded: $x \neq -2, 5$; LCD $= (x + 2)(x - 5)$
Multiply both sides by the LCD, then solve for x.
$x(x - 5) = x + 16$ $\Rightarrow$ $x = -2, x = 8$
$x^2 - 6x - 16 = 0$ $\quad$ Exclude –2.
$(x + 2)(x - 8) = 0$ $\quad$ $x = 8$

Note that the worked-out solutions do not restate the problems but rather show the subsequent steps.

FINAL EXAM ·································

1. Lesson 4
$5x - 3 = 7$
$5x = 10$
$x = 2$

2. Lessons 50 and 71
$f(3) = 8$
$f(0) = 1$
$f(3) - f(0) = 7$

3. Lesson 15
$m = \dfrac{1-4}{-3-2} = \dfrac{3}{5}$

4. Lesson 65
$\sqrt{36x^2} = 6x$

5. Lessons 80 and 81
$x^2 - 9 + x^2 - 6x + 9$
$= 2x^2 - 6x$

6. Lesson 19
D is a vertical line.

7. Lesson 6
$4x + 1 = -9$ or
$4x + 1 = 9$
$4x = -10$ or $4x = 8$
$x = -\dfrac{5}{2}$ or $x = 2$
$\left(-\dfrac{5}{2}\right) \times 2 = -5$

8. Lesson 23
Given $m = -1/3$
Perpendicular $m = 3$
$y = mx + b; (1, 5)$
$5 = 3(1) + b$
$b = 2$
$y = 3x + 2$

9. Lesson 33
k = −15 makes the two lines parallel.

10. Lesson 74
$x^{-5}y^{-4} \cdot 2^3 x^6 y^3 = 8xy^{-1} = \dfrac{8x}{y}$

11. Lesson 121
The vertex is at (1, 2):
$y = a(x - 1)^2 + 2$
Use (0, 1) to find a:
$1 = a(0 - 1)^2 + 2$
$1 = a + 2$
$a = -1$
Equation:
$y = -(x - 1)^2 + 2$

12. Lesson 40
$-11 \le 5 - 2x \le 11$
$-16 \le -2x \le 6$
$-3 \le x \le 8$

13. Lessons 50 and 111
$a^2 - 8 = 1$
$a^2 = 9$
$a = 3, a = -3$

14. Lesson 101
$4x^2(x + 2) - (x + 2)$
$= (x + 2)(4x^2 - 1)$
$= (x + 2)(2x + 1)(2x - 1)$

15. Lesson 111
$x^2 - 2x = 2$
$x^2 - 2x + 1 = 2 + 1$
$(x - 1)^2 = 3$
$x - 1 = \pm\sqrt{3}$
$x = 1 \pm \sqrt{3}$
The sum is 2.

16. Lesson 76
$3 + 4 + 3 = 10$

17. Lesson 22
Slope = −1
y-intercept = −2
$y = -x - 2$

18. Lesson 32
eq1 × 2 + eq2
$5x = 15$
$x = 3$
$2(3) + y = 5$
$y = -1$
Solution: (3, −1)

19. Lesson 68
$4\sqrt{x + 1} = 8$
$\sqrt{x + 1} = 2$
Square both sides.
$x + 1 = 4$
$x = 3$

20. Lessons 95, 99, and 125
$\dfrac{(x - 1)^2}{(x - 1)(x + 3)}$
$= \dfrac{x - 1}{x + 3}$

21. Lessons 118 and 119
Intercept form:
$y = (x - 2)(x + 5)$
x-intercepts: 2, −5
Distance = 2 − (−5) = 7

22. Lesson 20
A has a vertex at (1, 0).

23. Lesson 128
Excluded: $x \ne -2, 3$; LCD $= 2(x + 2)(x - 3)$
Multiply both sides by the LCD, then solve for x.
$2(x - 3) + 4(x + 2) = (x + 2)(x - 3)$
$x^2 - 7x - 8 = 0$
$(x + 1)(x - 8) = 0$
$x = -1, x = 8$

24. Lesson 56
Use $y = kx$.
$10 = 8k$, so $k = 5/4$.
$y = (5/4)12 = 15$
15 feet long

25. Lesson 9
x = number of nickels
$x + 3$ = number of dimes
$0.1(x + 3) + 0.05x = 1.05$
Solve for x, and $x = 5$.
5 nickels and 8 dimes

26. Lesson 130
x = Eli's time alone
$\dfrac{1}{10} + \dfrac{1}{x} = \dfrac{1}{6}$
$x = 15$
15 hours

27. Lessons 22 and 41
Line: $y = 2x + 1$
Dashed: > or <
Use any point to determine the direction.
$y > 2x + 1$

28. Lesson 26
Rate of change = −9 − 11
Initial value = 300
$y = -20x + 300$

29. Lesson 10
t = time to meet
$60t + 65t = 250$; $t = 2$
2 hours

30. Lesson 34
x = # of 4-seat tables
y = # of 6-seat tables
$x + y = 20$, $4x + 6y = 90$
$x = 15, y = 5$
15 4-seat tables
5 6-seat tables

31. Lesson 51
C is exponential, not linear.

32. Lesson 113

   x = width

   $10 - x$ = height

   $x(10 - x) = 24$

   $x = 4, x = 6$

   4 inches by 6 inches

33. Lesson 11

   x = liters of 25% solution

   $0.25x + 0.4(4) = 0.3(x + 4)$

   $x = 8$

   8 liters of 25% solution

34. Lesson 149

   3 independent events

   P = 1/2 × 1/2 × 1/2

   The probability is 1/8.

35. Lesson 58

   Arithmetic sequence

   $a_1 = 5, d = 7$

   $a_n = 7n - 2$

   $a_{15} = 7(15) - 2 = 103$

36. Lesson 123

   $h(t) = -16(t + 1)(t - 4)$

   $h = 0$ at $t = -1$ and $t = 4$

   4 seconds

37. Lesson 113

   $8^2 + x^2 = 17^2$; $x = 15$

   The other leg is 15 cm.

   The perimeter is 40 cm.

38. Lesson 78

   Exponential growth

   $y = 10(2)^x$

   3 hours = 9 x 20 minutes

   When $x = 9$, $y = 5120$.

   5,120 bacteria

39. Lesson 144

   64/77 = 0.83116...

   About 83% of the teens

40. Lesson 154

   Total possible outcomes = P(6, 6)

   Favorable outcomes = permutations of 5 remaining books after math is placed in the first position = P(5, 5)

   Probability $= \dfrac{P(5,5)}{P(6,6)} = \dfrac{5!}{6!} = \dfrac{1}{6}$

Made in the USA
Las Vegas, NV
17 July 2023